Foreign Investment in Copper Mining

Foreign Investment in Copper Mining

Case Studies of Mines in Peru and Papua New Guinea

Raymond F. Mikesell

Published for
RESOURCES FOR THE FUTURE, INC.
by THE JOHNS HOPKINS UNIVERSITY PRESS
Baltimore and London

Contents

Preface   ***xiii***

Acknowledgments   ***xv***

Introduction   ***xvii***
    A SUMMARY OF FINDINGS   xviii

I. Investment Decision Making and Contract Negotiation in Copper Mining

1. *An Introduction to Investment Decision Making and Contract Negotiation*   3
    PROFITABILITY   3
    Measures of Profitability   5
    CASH FLOW ANALYSIS   6
    Calculation of Cash Flow and Rates of Return   7
    TECHNICAL AND ECONOMIC FACTORS IN CASH FLOW ANALYSIS   13
    Price Projections   15
    Forward Contracts and Sales to Affiliates   16
    THE MINIMUM EXPECTED RATE OF RETURN   17
    POLITICAL RISKS   18
    OTHER FACTORS IN INVESTMENT DECISIONS   20
    METHODS OF FINANCING   21
    The Trend Toward High Debt-Equity Ratios   24

NEGOTIATING THE CONTRACT TERMS   24
LIVING UNDER A MINE
DEVELOPMENT AGREEMENT   29
Conflict and Relative Bargaining Strength   31
Can Conflict Be Reduced?   32
HOST COUNTRY BENEFITS FROM
FOREIGN MINING INVESTMENT   34

II.   The Toquepala and Bougainville Mines: Case Histories in the Economics of Copper Mining

2. *A Brief History of the Toquepala Project   39*
DISCOVERY AND EXPLORATION   39
NEGOTIATIONS WITH THE
EXPORT–IMPORT BANK   40
NEGOTIATION OF THE
CONCESSION AGREEMENT   44
CAPITAL REQUIREMENTS AND THE
MOBILIZATION OF FUNDS   47
THE PRODUCTION PERIOD   48
Marketing of Products   51
The Cuajone Bilateral Agreement   51
CUAJONE AND QUELLAVECO   53
Cuajone   53
Quellaveco   55
THE SYSTEM OF MINING
COMMUNITIES   55

3. *Economic and Political Factors in the Investment Decision for the Toquepala Project   57*
PROJECTING FUTURE COPPER PRICES   59
ESTIMATING COSTS AND
CAPITAL REQUIREMENTS   61
PROJECTED PROFITABILITY OF
TOQUEPALA   62

CONTENTS vii

4. Contribution of the Toquepala Mine to the Peruvian Economy   66
GROSS REVENUES AND
RETAINED VALUE   66
The Sharing of Before-Tax Earnings   69
OTHER IMPACTS ON THE
PERUVIAN ECONOMY   70
Foreign Exchange Impact   70
Impact on Employment   70
*Expenditures for Peruvian Goods
and Services   71*
The Resource Impact   71

5. Financial Analysis of Toquepala   72
RETURNS TO ORIGINAL
STOCKHOLDERS   72
The Accounting Rate of Return   75

**6. A Brief History of the
Bougainville Mine   78**
DISCOVERY AND EXPLORATION   78
THE BOUGAINVILLE COPPER
PROJECT AGREEMENT   80
Leases and Royalties   82
Government Equity Participation   83
Import Duties   83
Taxation   83
Government Investment Undertakings   85
Provisions Relating to the Bougainvillians   86
*Local Purchases and the Hiring and Training
of Local Personnel   87*
Processing the Ore   87
Expropriation and Arbitration   87
RENEGOTIATION OF THE BCP
AGREEMENT IN 1974   88
CAPITAL STRUCTURE OF BCP   88
THE BEGINNING OF COMMERCIAL
OPERATIONS   90

7. *Factors in the Investment Decision for the Bougainville Mine* **92**
THE PROJECT EVALUATION 92
ESTIMATING PROFITABILITY OF THE
BOUGAINVILLE PROJECT 95
NONECONOMIC FACTORS IN
THE INVESTMENT DECISION 98

8. *The Economic Contribution of the Bougainville Mine to PNG* **100**
THE ECONOMIC IMPACT DURING
THE CONSTRUCTION PERIOD 100
Impact on Employment 100
Agricultural Impact 102
THE AMOUNT AND DISTRIBUTION
OF RETAINED VALUE 104
RETAINED VALUE FOR
APRIL 1972–DECEMBER 1973 105
Retained Value for a Representative Year (1983) 107
Retained Value During the Construction Period 108
BCL'S CONTRIBUTION TO THE
BALANCE OF PAYMENTS AND
NATIONAL PRODUCT 109
THE FISCAL IMPACT ON THE
PNG GOVERNMENT 111
PNG Revenues from BCL 112
Analysis of the BCL Tax Regime Under the 1967 Agreement 113
Comparison with the Tax Regime Under the 1974 Agreement 114
PNG Government Outlays Related to BCL 115
EMPLOYMENT AND TRAINING 117
CONTRIBUTION OF THE MINE TO
DOMESTIC PRODUCTION 119
Backward and Forward Linkages 120

9. *Financial Returns to BCL Equity Investors: A Simulation Analysis* **122**

**10. Renegotiating the Bougainville Mine
Agreement   127**
PRELIMINARY PROPOSALS FOR
RENEGOTIATION   128
RENEGOTIATION OF THE
1967 AGREEMENT   130

**Appendix A. The Calculation of the
Internal Rate of Return   133**

**Appendix B. Comparison of Agreements
for Projects in Indonesia,
Botswana, and Papua
New Guinea   135**

Index   139

TABLES

CHAPTER 1

1. Cash Flow for a Hypothetical Mine, Assuming an Investment of $100 Million Over a Five-Year Construction Period and a Fifteen-Year Operating Life   8
2. Net Cash Flow to Equity and Accounting Rate of Return to Initial Equity Investment Assuming Straightline Depreciation   9
3. Net Cash Flow to Equity and Accounting Rate of Return to Initial Equity, Assuming Accelerated Depreciation   10

CHAPTER 2

4. Production, Cost, and Price Data for Toquepala, 1960–73   49
5. Days Lost from Strikes at the Toquepala Mine and at the Smelter in Ilo, 1966–73   50

CHAPTER 3

6. Annual Average of U.S. Domestic Producers' and London Metal Exchange Copper Prices, 1938–73   60

CHAPTER 4

7. Distribution of Toquepala Gross Revenue, 1960–72   68
8. Distribution of Retained Value Generated by Toquepala, 1960–72   69

CHAPTER 5

9. Toquepala: Cash Flow to Majority Equity Stockholders and Internal Rates of Return (IRR), 1944–79   74

CHAPTER 7

10. Projected Financial Returns to CRA–NBHC Equity Investment for Alternative Prices of Copper   97

CHAPTER 8

11. Distribution of BCL's Total Revenue (R) and Retained Value (RV) Components During April 1, 1972–December 31, 1973   106
12. Simulated Revenues, Expenditures, and Distribution of Earnings of BCL for a Representative Year (1983)   108

13. Simulated Distribution of BCL Revenues for A Representative
     Year (1983): Retained Value and External Payments   109
14. Direct BCL Contributions to the PNG Government in 1973, and
     for a Representative Year (1983)   112
15. Operation of the PNG Tax Arrangement for BCL   114
16. Projected PNG Government Capital Outlays and Borrowings
     Related to the Bougainville Mine   116
17. Percentage of Indigenous Workers in Each Skill Category, as of
     1972, and as Projected for 1975 and 1980   118

CHAPTER 9

18. Simulation of Cash Flow to Equity Stockholders in BCL   125

APPENDIX B

B–1. Summary of Terms of Three Project Agreements   136

FIGURE

1. Effect of BCL Activity on the Agricultural Sphere in Papua
    New Guinea   103

Preface

The construction of a large modern mine in a developing country is a long process. At several stages decisions must be made whether to go forward or to terminate the endeavor, and at each stage a large number of technical, economic, and political factors enter into the decision. The existence of an ore body may be known for decades or even centuries, but whether it provides the technical and economic basis for a mine that is at once capable of producing income for the host country and foreign investor, and of being a source of needed materials for the world cannot be known without a large expenditure of capital and human effort over many years. Until this effort is made and the fundamental questions answered favorably, the ore body has no value beyond the environment in which it may be found. Although the history of every mine is unique, the case histories of two of the world's largest copper mines—the Bougainville mine in Papua New Guinea and the Toquepala mine in Peru—illustrate many of the problems encountered in the creation of a mine in an isolated area of a nonindustrialized country, one a rain forest and the other a desert.

Two types of literature have in recent years touched on the matter of mineral resource exploitation: studies dealing with development and growth and speculative analyses of the long-term outlook for resource adequacy. Rarely are the considerations that must go into a decision to invest in a mine costing several hundred million dollars fully appreciated—neither by social scientists who write about foreign investment and its impact on developing countries, nor by those who foresee the "end of the line." A better understanding of these issues as they relate to the foreign investment policies of the host countries and to the negotiation and implementation of mine development agreements between host countries and foreign mining companies is essential if world output of minerals is to expand in the most economical manner for meeting world requirements, and if mineral exporting countries are to reap the maximum social gains from the development of their resources. It is equally important to understand the nature of the economic and social impact of foreign investment in minerals on the host country; these impacts are analyzed quantitatively in the two case histories covered in this volume.

This study, while emphasizing the investment decision process, is a sequel to *Foreign Investment in the Petroleum and Mineral Industries: Case Studies in Investor–Host Country Relations,* by Raymond F. Mikesell and his associates, published in 1971 by the Johns Hopkins University Press for Resources for the Future. For the past three years the author has been visiting copper mines in Africa, Australia, South America, and the South Pacific for the purpose of interviewing officials of mining companies and host governments who are concerned with the formulation and implementation of foreign investment policies in the mineral industries. This study constitutes a portion of the author's continuing research on the world copper industry outside the United States, which has been supported by Resources for the Future, Inc.

July 1975

Hans H. Landsberg
Director
Division of Energy and
Resource Commodities
Resources for the Future, Inc.

Acknowledgments

This study constitutes a portion of a long-range investigation of the world copper industry with emphasis on the contribution of developed countries to the supply of copper. It owes its inspiration and initial support to the late Orris C. Herfindahl, formerly a senior research associate, and Sam H. Schurr, formerly director of the Mineral Resources Program at Resources for the Future. This study has been financed in large part by a grant from Resources for the Future, Inc. to the University of Oregon.

The two case histories could not have been written without the very generous cooperation of officials of the Southern Peru Copper Corporation (SPCC) and Bougainville Copper Ltd. (BCL), who provided their time for interviews and the preparation of extended written answers to questions and supplied the author with virtually every available company document that was relevant to the study. Information was also provided by officials of the governments where the mines are located. The author is especially indebted to Frank Archibald, chairman of the SPCC; Charles F. Barber, chairman of the American Smelting and Refining Company (ASARCO), and Stephen P. McCandless, assistant treasurer of ASARCO, for assistance on the Toquepala case history; and to Ray W. Ballmer, managing director, Alan McCallum, manager for finance, and Don. C. Vernon, general manager of the mine, for assistance on the Bougainville case study. The author was afforded every hospitality during his visits to the sites of the two mines, and on the occasion of his visits to the main offices of the SPCC and BCL in New York City and Melbourne, Australia, respectively.

Although officials of both mining companies were given the opportunity to comment on the manuscript for purposes of checking the accuracy of the material presented, they did not place any restrictions on the subject matter covered or on any judgments or conclusions. In any case, the author takes sole responsibility for all of the empirical information and analysis found in this study.

June 1975   Raymond F. Mikesell
                                                   University of Oregon

Introduction

This study is in two parts. Part I presents the basic factors in the decision to invest in a foreign mining operation and their relationship to the negotiation of mine development contracts with the governments of host countries. Particular attention is given to the measure and determination of the profitability of a prospective mining venture and to the minimum expected rate of return and other conditions necessary to induce an investment in mining in a developing country.

Part II presents case studies of two of the world's largest open-pit copper mines: Southern Peru Copper Corporation's Toquepala mine, which began operations in 1960, and the Bougainville mine in Papua New Guinea (PNG), controlled by Conzinc Riotinto of Australia (CRA), which began operations in 1972. The case studies analyze the various considerations leading to the initial decisions to invest and the factors determining the methods of financing. Both case studies discuss the negotiation of the mine development agreements with the host countries and subsequent issues arising between the companies and the host governments under the agreements. Contract negotiations and demands for contract renegotiation are greatly influenced by what the host country receives or expects to receive from the operations of the mine. Therefore, the case studies include an analysis of the contributions of the mines to the economies of the host countries as well as of the division of the economic rents between the companies and the host countries. Each of the studies concludes with a financial analysis of the mine and a calculation of the rates of return on stockholders' equity, using alternative methods of assessing profitability.

In the preparation of these case studies I have received generous assistance from company officials, and much of the information contained in the studies has been drawn from company records and from interviews with personnel both at the offices of the parent companies and at the mines.

A SUMMARY OF FINDINGS

The two case studies in Part II show the application of the principles of investment decision making and contract negotiation, which are set forth in Part I, and analyze the economic results of the investments. Obviously, it is dangerous to generalize or to confirm hypotheses from the observations generated by only two case studies. Nevertheless, studies of two successful mining operations in two developing countries reveal problems and approaches to their resolution that may have application to other mining ventures.

A brief survey of the findings which have general implications for foreign mining investment in developing countries is given in the paragraphs which follow.

In the case of both the Toquepala and the Bougainville mines, the period of exploration, mine evaluation, and project formulation was marked by great uncertainties with respect to the economic feasibility of the mine, the cost of bringing the mine into production, and the mobilization of capital for the investment. In the case of Toquepala, over $12 million was spent over a ten-year period before a final decision was made in late 1955 to construct the mine; while in the case of Bougainville, over A$21 million was spent over a five-year period before the final investment decision was made in late 1969.[1] The construction cost of the Toquepala mine was 40 percent above the initial estimate, while the cost of the Bougainville mine was more than 250 percent above the initial estimate. These were not cost overruns, but rather reflected increases in cost estimates arising from information generated during the period of mine evaluation and project formulation. Both mines produce low-grade ores, and both involved geological, engineering, and environmental conditions that were unique, requiring innovations and previously untried procedures. The high construction cost of the mines ($237 million for Toquepala and over A$350 million for Bougainville) necessitated the mobilization of large amounts of debt capital and substantially more equity capital than had been originally envisaged. The arrangements of bank loans and suppliers' credits required assurances to the creditors of a market for the product over the maturities of the loans, and special conditions to assure that the proceeds from the sale of the product would be available for the debt service. In the case of Toquepala, a market for the product could be assured by the requirements of the vertically integrated parent

[1] A$ represents Australian dollars. In 1969 A$1 = U.S.$1.12. In 1971 the value of the Australian dollar rose to U.S.$1.19; and since September 1973 its value has been U.S.$1.49.

companies. In the case of Bougainville, long-term contracts for the bulk of the output were made with foreign purchasers.

Economic feasibility of the mines depended substantially on the long-run outlook for the price of copper. Projecting the future price of copper was especially difficult for the investment decision in Toquepala, since during the early planning period in 1952–53 copper prices reflected the increased demand arising from the Korean War, but a decline to the level of prices in the immediate post-World War II period would have rendered the project financially unfeasible. During the planning period of the Bougainville mine, the London Metal Exchange (LME) price for copper ranged from 30 U.S. cents per pound to 70 U.S. cents per pound, but the project could not have been profitable at the lower price range. For both projects, the final decision to undertake the investment was made on the basis of price projections that in retrospect appear to have been very conservative. Also, for both mines, the expected rates of return indicated that the mines would be only marginally profitable. In other words, the project initiators did not believe they had a bonanza. Basically, their belief in the viability of the projects rested on confidence in world economic growth and a reasonable degree of prosperity.

The investment climate in the host country and the encouragement and cooperation of the government of the foreign investor played a decisive role in the investment decisions relating to both mines. In the mid-1950s Peru was politically and economically stable, and the government was exceedingly anxious for the investment in Toquepala to be made. The project initiator of Toquepala, the American Smelting and Refining Company (ASARCO), regarded a loan from the U.S. government as an essential condition for the construction of the mine. Although the interest of the U.S. government vacillated during the planning period for Toquepala, the final decision on the Export–Import Bank loan to finance the mine was made in 1955 on both political and economic grounds. In the case of the Bougainville mine, however, the investment decision was made on the expectation that PNG would continue to be a dependency of Australia for at least a decade following the construction of the mine. In addition, the Australian government was anxious for the mine to be constructed, and this attitude was reflected both in the negotiation of the mine development agreement with the government and in their indirect financial assistance for the project. In both Peru and PNG, the investment climate has deteriorated rapidly since the mines went into operation. Taxes have risen substantially in Peru, and the government has adopted a policy of nationalization with respect to mining, although Toquepala itself has not been expropriated. PNG became self-governing in 1973, the year following the beginning of operations of the Bougainville mine, and in 1974 government leaders demanded renegotiation of the 1969 mine development contract. Had these changes in the investment climate been anticipated by the foreign investors, it is doubtful whether either of these mines would have been constructed.

Both mines were heavily financed with borrowed funds, since the project initiators were unwilling to provide equity capital running to hundreds of millions of dollars. The debt–equity ratio was 6:1 for Toquepala (including advances by the partners as debt) and 2:1 for the Bougainville mine. Thus, a substantial proportion of the gross operating profits (gross revenues minus direct operating expenses) was required for debt service during the early years of operations. During a period of large debt service, taxes and dividends combined must ordinarily constitute a relatively small proportion of gross operating profits. Under these conditions, accelerated depreciation or reduced taxes are usually necessary in order to provide sufficient cash flow for debt service if any profits are going to be available for distribution to equity holders. (Investors are unlikely to be interested in providing equity capital for mines if, after a construction period of five years or more, they must wait an additional seven or eight years before receiving a return on their investment.) In the case of Toquepala, profits transferred abroad and income taxes paid to the government totaled U.S. $60 million and U.S. $30 million, respectively, for the first six years of operations (1960–65), but debt service amounted to U.S. $199 million. However, during the period 1966–72 debt service was only U.S. $30 million, profits transferred abroad were $221 million (plus U.S. $78 million in profits reinvested in the Cuajone mine), and income taxes paid to the Peruvian government totaled U.S. $232 million. The Bougainville mine has not been in operation long enough to compare financial results during and after the period of large debt service. However, during the initial period of operations, April 1, 1972–December 31, 1973, debt service plus the additions to cash reserves required by the credit agreement totaled A$157 million, as contrasted with A$61 million in dividends paid to private equity holders and A$33 million in withholding taxes, royalties, and dividends paid to the PNG government.

The financial analysis of the operations of the two mines reveals the inappropriateness of the accounting rate of return to equity as normally calculated—that is, the ratio of net earnings before taxes to book value minus depreciation—as a basis for measuring profitability.

The long period of investment before operations begin combined with the long period during which the bulk of the net earnings plus capital consumption allowances must be used for payments on debt principal may extend the period when substantial returns to equity are realized. Following the period of debt repayment, what may appear to be a very high accounting rate of return on net book value may in fact constitute a very low internal rate of return (discounted cash flow). In the case of the Toquepala mine, for example, all of the initial investment, including both equity and borowings, had been returned through capital consumption allowances (depreciation, amortization, and depletion) by 1967–68, so that in a sense there was no net book value thereafter. Nevertheless, the internal rate of return to equity was 13.6 percent in current prices through 1972 (after taking account of liquidation value), and about 12.3 percent in 1972 prices. A projection of the cash flow to equity through 1979, based on recent earnings, would increase the internal rate of return to about 15 percent in terms of current prices and to about 14 percent in terms of 1972 prices.

The case studies show that following the period of debt repayment half or more of the gross revenues from the sale of the products of the mine have been retained in the host country. In the case of the Toquepala mine, retained value (payments to the government and to domestic labor plus domestic purchases of goods and services) absorbed about 49 percent of the gross revenues from the sale of the products, and 23 percent constituted profits transferred abroad. The remaining 28 percent was largely accounted for by imports and debt service. In the case of the Bougainville mine, for a representative period in the future (1983) retained value is estimated to constitute 62 percent of gross revenues, and dividends transferred abroad about 22 percent. For Toquepala during the 1966–72 period, government taxes constituted about 30 percent of gross revenues, while in the case of the Bougainville mine for the projected representative year in the future (1983), government revenue is projected to constitute about 45 percent of gross revenues. The higher proportion of government revenue for Bougainville reflects in considerable measure the 20 percent equity interest of the PNG government in Bougainville Copper Limited (BCL).

The major benefits to the host countries from the foreign investment in the extractive industries arise from government tax revenues rather than from payments to labor and for goods and services. Peru is the more advanced of the two developing countries, and a larger proportion of the labor and material inputs was supplied by domestic sources in that country than was the case in PNG.

The two case studies confirm the generalization that conflicts between the host government and the foreign investor tend to be more or less continuous, and the greater the profitability of the mine the more intense will be the demand for renegotiation of the contract on the part of the host government. The bargaining strength of the foreign investor will be greatest at the time when the foreign company is considering a substantial increase in investment. This is well illustrated by the relatively favorable treatment given by the Peruvian government to the Southern Peru Copper Company (SPCC), as compared with its treatment of other large foreign mining firms in Peru during the period in which the SPCC was constructing and mobilizing the capital for an investment of over $600 million in the Cuajone mine. On the other hand, renegotiation of the 1967 Bougainville mine agreement was demanded within two years of the initiation of commercial production, and the PNG government achieved an increase in taxes that reduced by more than half the dividends of the foreign investors.

The frequent demands for renegotiation of long-term mining contracts suggest that conflict might be reduced by the inclusion in mine development contracts of a provision whereby certain conditions would be open for renegotiation, say, every five to eight years following the recovery of the capital investment. Such provisions, however, should include guidelines regarding what is negotiable, and a limitation on changes in conditions that would reduce the company's internal rate of return below an agreed level.

I
Investment Decision Making and Contract Negotiation in Copper Mining

1
An Introduction to Investment Decision Making and Contract Negotiation

Part I of this study identifies the major economic factors influencing investment decisions in copper mining (and in metal mining generally), and shows their relationship to mine development contracts with host governments. No attempt has been made here to formulate a specialized theory of the behavior of mining firms. The major economic factors governing investment decisions are based mainly on empirical evidence gathered from unpublished documents and from interviews with officials of mining companies. Both the weights given to various factors, such as expected rates of return, risk, and control of product supply, and the degree of sophistication in applying a given set of investment criteria differ substantially from company to company. Given the same information, no two companies are likely to come up with the same evaluation of a project, and, even if they did, the actual decision would reflect circumstances internal to the companies themselves. Nevertheless, the following review will identify those factors governing investment decisions that are taken account of in a greater or lesser degree by virtually all copper mining companies contemplating an investment in a developing country.

PROFITABILITY

Establishing the profitability of a mine project, even apart from any consideration of economic and political risks (which will be considered in the sections entitled "Technical and Economic Factors in Cash Flow Analysis" and "Political Risks") is a complicated process. It involves an estimation of the grade composition of the ore body, the cost of mining, hauling, milling, smelting, and refining, the long-run price of the product, and the effects of the tax arrangements on cash flow. Competent and thorough engineering evaluation can yield reasonably reliable production cost estimates based on existing prices, but the price of labor and other domestic inputs, the exchange rate, and world prices of imported equipment and materials can vary sharply over the relevant period for estimating profits. Nevertheless, since operating costs tend to parallel rates of inflation in the host country and in the world generally, and differences in relative rates of inflation among countries tend to be offset by changes in exchange rates, operating costs are more readily estimated than are product prices which are subject to extreme short-term swings with changes in demand-and-supply conditions.

In estimating profitability it is necessary to project prices or price trends twenty-five or thirty years in the future. Most new copper mines require four to six years to construct after the investment decision is made. The existence of large debt financing, requiring heavy debt service payments for ten to fifteen years after production is initiated, emphasizes the importance of the price projections over the first fifteen or twenty years following the investment decision. As will be noted in the case studies, mining firms employ a variety of approaches for projecting copper prices. In recent years a rash of new econometric models has been formulated for projecting the demand for and supply of copper and the prices of copper in different markets, but their reliability over the older rule-of-thumb methods (which were not very reliable) is yet to be demonstrated. Relatively good projections of world mine capacity over a five-year period can be made, but this is because the bulk of the new capacity five years hence has already been planned. But the amount of new capacity, designed to come on-stream five years in the future, will depend upon a host of factors, including not only price trends in the interim, but taxes and investment climate in the host country, new discoveries, ownership patterns, technology, the cost and availability of financing, and anticipated demand for the product. The long-run projection of copper prices being made by firms today will probably be wide of the mark, but what those projections are is vital for investment decisions which determine the volume of copper-producing capacity five years from now.

Measures of Profitability

The internal rate of return or discounted cash flow (DCF) approach to the evaluation of profitability has been part of the literature on mining economics for more than two decades, and the method of mine valuation by discounting future income has been in the literature at least since the first appearance of the Hoskold formula for mine valuation in 1877.[1] However, until recently many large mining firms were not employing the DCF criterion in evaluating mine projects. This point is well illustrated in the case study of Toquepala (see page 58).

Today most mining firms estimate the profitability of a project by projecting cash outflow during the construction period and net cash inflow over the expected life of the mine or for the period of the mine contract or another arbitrarily determined period, and then calculating that rate of interest which equates the discounted or present value of cash outflow with the discounted value of cash inflow.[2] The fact that officials in many host governments continue to calculate profits in terms of the accounting rate of return, that is, the ratio of net earnings to net book value, has often led to misunderstanding and controversy over the actual profitability of a mine to the equity holders.[3] The difficulty with the accounting rate of return is that it fails to take into account the long period of mine exploration, evaluation, and construction during which the investor receives no return on his investment.

In recent years some government officials of developing countries have begun to think in terms of the DCF and are preparing their own cash flow analyses, based either on data derived from the company or from information generated by their own mining engineers. To cite an example, when Kennecott Pacific Pty. Ltd., a subsidiary of the

[1] See H. D. Hoskold, *The Engineer's Valuing Assistant, or a Practical Treatise on the Valuation of Collieries and Other Mines* (2nd ed., 1905, London: Longmans, Green, 1877). Despite its drawbacks, mining firms still use the Hoskold formula. For a criticism, see D. H. Eldridge, "Is Use of the Hoskold Formula Justified?", *Engineering and Mining Journal* (August 1949), pp. 72–74.

[2] See Appendix A, for the method of calculating the internal rate of return of the DCF.

[3] For a mathematical analysis of the relationship between the internal rate of return and the accounting rate of return, see Ezra Solomon, "Alternative Rate of Return Concepts and Their Implications for Utility Regulations," *The Bell Journal of Economics and Management Science* (Spring 1970), pp. 65–81; see also, Thomas R. Stauffer, "The Measurement of Corporate Rates of Return: A Generalized Formulation," *The Bell Journal of Economics and Management Science* (Autumn 1971), pp. 434–469.

Kennecott Copper Corporation, presented a preliminary evaluation and cash flow projection for the Ok Tedi copper project in Northeast Papua to the PNG government in August 1972, the PNG Ministry of Mines prepared its own cash flow projections on different assumptions regarding the method of financing and other variables, and calculated the DCF corresponding to each alternative set of assumptions. Under the Ministry of Mines' assumptions, the DCF was substantially higher than that calculated in the evaluation presented by Kennecott.[4]

CASH FLOW ANALYSIS

Cash flow analysis in the evaluation of the profitability of a mine involves an estimation of capital expenditures (cash outflow) prior to the beginning of production, and a projection of cash inflow minus capital expenditures after production is initiated. We may define gross cash flow (GCF) following the construction period as:

$$GCF = R - C - I - T$$

where
  R = revenues from operations
  C = operating costs
  I = interest on indebtedness
  T = tax payments.

Included in the GCF are depreciation, amortization, and depletion (where permitted). These items constitute the capital consumption allowances permitted under the tax regulations for the calculation of taxable income.

Net cash flow (NCF) may be defined as follows:

$$NCF = R - C - I - T - L - CE$$

where
  CE = capital expenditures necessary to maintain output
  L = principal payments on debt.

NCF is available for distribution to the equity holders or may be added to cash reserves. For any category of equity holders, cash flow over a given period will be determined by the equity investment (cash outflow) and the dividends received (cash inflow). It is important to

4 See Raymond F. Mikesell, *Foreign Investment in Copper Mining in Papua New Guinea: Current Developments and Prospects,* External Research Study, U.S. Department of State (September 1973), pp. 15–17.

distinguish between cash flow to equity and earnings after taxes. Earnings after taxes (Y) may be defined as:

$$Y = R - C - I - D - T = TI - T$$

where

D = capital consumption allowances (depreciation, amortization, and depletion)

TI = taxable income.

It is important to note that earnings after taxes can be greater or less than NCF to equity. Thus, if there are no principal payments on the debt (L), and capital expenditures necessary to maintain production are less than capital consumption allowances (D), NCF to equity can be larger than earnings after taxes (Y). However, during a period when debt repayments are high, NCF to equity may be less than earnings after taxes, and dividends will be limited to NCF minus additions to cash reserves. Moreover, during this period gross capital flow must be large enough to assure that sufficient funds are available to provide for debt repayments and the necessary capital expenditures to maintain production.[5]

Calculation of Cash Flow and Rates of Return

Depreciation. Table 1 provides illustrative cash flow data for a hypothetical mine, representing an investment of $100 million over a five-year period and having a productive life of fifteen years. Tables 2 and 3 provide an illustration of the effects of accelerated depreciation on the internal rate of return to equity (DCF) and a comparison of the internal rates of return with the accounting rate of return to initial equity. In Table 1, it is assumed that the initial investment of $100 million is financed in equal amounts by equity and loan capital. The debt is repayable during the first ten years of operations at 8 percent per annum, plus accumulated interest during the construction period, payable in the first year of operations. To simplify the calculation, it is assumed that the entire $100 million investment is in the form of depreciable assets. In Table 2, taxable income is calculated on the basis of straightline depreciation over the fifteen-year operating period,

---

[5] Capital expenditures undertaken for a major expansion of the mine may be considered as a part of net cash inflow to equity, since ordinarily the company may choose between paying NCF to equity to shareholders in the form of dividends or reinvesting these funds in the enterprise. Usually, reinvested earnings are regarded as those amounts invested in excess of capital consumption allowances, but ordinarily the total amount of capital consumption allowances does not need to be reinvested in the enterprise but may be paid out in dividends.

Table 1. Cash Flow for a Hypothetical Mine, Assuming an Investment of $100 Million Over a Five-Year Construction Period and a Fifteen-Year Operating Life
(millions of dollars)

Year	Gross revenue (R)	Operating costs (C)	Equity outflow (E)	Loans and principal repayments (L)	Interest payments on debt (I)	Postconstruction capital expenditures (CE)
1	—	—	10	10	—	—
2	—	—	10	10	—	—
3	—	—	10	10	—	—
4	—	—	10	10	—	—
5	—	—	10	10	—	—
6	50	(20)	—	(5)	(13.4)	(2)
7	50	(20)	—	(5)	(3.6)	(2)
8	50	(20)	—	(5)	(3.2)	(2)
9	50	(20)	—	(5)	(2.8)	(2)
10	50	(20)	—	(5)	(2.4)	(2)
11	50	(20)	—	(5)	(2.0)	(2)
12	50	(20)	—	(5)	(1.6)	(2)
13	50	(20)	—	(5)	(1.2)	(2)
14	50	(20)	—	(5)	(0.8)	(2)
15	50	(20)	—	(5)	(0.4)	(2)
16	50	(20)	—	—	—	(2)
17	50	(20)	—	—	—	(2)
18	50	(20)	—	—	—	(2)
19	50	(20)	—	—	—	(2)
20	50	(20)	—	—	—	(2)

Note: Numbers in parentheses designate cash outflow in millions of dollars.

while in Table 3, taxable income is calculated on the basis of accelerated depreciation. The company pays a tax of 50 percent on taxable income.

On the basis of straightline depreciation, NCF to equity is relatively low over the first ten years of operation, during which time the service payments on debt are made. Equity outlays are not recouped until the sixth year of operation or eleven years after the initiation of construction. Assuming accelerated depreciation, the initial equity capital is virtually recouped after three years of operation. Under straightline depreciation, the internal rate of return to initial equity is 13.5 percent, less than the minimum expected rate of return which is usually necessary to attract equity capital in mining. With accelerated depreciation, the internal rate of return to initial equity is 16.6 percent. It will be observed that the mean accounting rate of return to initial equity over the fifteen years of operations is 21.2 percent in the case of both straightline and accelerated depreciation, but there is no taxable income in the first four years under accelerated depreciation.

Table 2. Net Cash Flow to Equity and Accounting Rate of Return to Initial Equity Investment, Assuming Straightline Depreciation (millions of dollars)

Year	Depreciation (D)	Taxable income (TI)	Tax payments (T)	Earnings after taxes[a] (Y)	Net cash flow to equity[b] (NCF)	Accounting rate of return to initial equity (%)
1	—	—	—	—	(10)	—
2	—	—	—	—	(10)	—
3	—	—	—	—	(10)	—
4	—	—	—	—	(10)	—
5	—	—	—	—	(10)	—
6	6.7	9.9	4.9	5.0	4.7	9.9
7	6.7	19.7	9.8	9.9	9.6	19.7
8	6.7	20.1	10.0	10.1	9.8	20.1
9	6.7	20.5	10.2	10.3	10.0	20.5
10	6.7	20.9	10.4	10.5	10.2	20.9
11	6.7	21.3	10.6	10.7	10.4	21.3
12	6.7	21.7	10.8	10.9	10.6	21.7
13	6.7	22.1	11.0	11.1	10.8	22.1
14	6.7	22.5	11.2	11.3	11.0	22.5
15	6.7	22.9	11.4	11.5	11.2	22.9
16	6.7	23.3	11.6	11.7	11.4	23.3
17	6.7	23.3	11.6	11.7	11.4	23.3
18	6.7	23.3	11.6	11.7	11.4	23.3
19	6.7	23.3	11.6	11.7	11.4	23.3
20	6.7	23.3	11.6	11.7	11.4	23.3

Notes: Numbers in parentheses designate cash outflow in millions of dollars.
Internal rate of return to initial equity equals 13.5 percent.
Mean accounting rate of return to initial equity equals 21.2 percent.
[a] Assumes 50 percent tax on taxable income (TI):
$$TI = R - C - I - D$$
$$Y = TI - T$$
where T = tax payments.
[b] $NCF = R - C - I - T - L - CE$. During the first five years NCF represents equity outflow.

A higher cash flow in the early period of operations can also be achieved by a tax holiday, and in the case of the Bougainville copper project agreement there was a three-year tax holiday followed by accelerated depreciation, resulting in an extended period of tax exemption. Although the immediate effect of a tax holiday and of accelerated depreciation is the same, that is, no taxable income for a given period, accelerated depreciation results eventually in higher taxable income and, hence, higher taxes in the period following the full depreciation of the initial investment as compared with the situation following a tax holiday with straightline depreciation. Therefore, some mining companies make accounting provision for a "deferred tax," which is an amount equal to the tax that would have been paid if the

Table 3. Net Cash Flow to Equity and Accounting Rate of Return
to Initial Equity, Assuming Accelerated Depreciation
(millions of dollars)

Year	Depreciation (D)	Taxable income (TI)	Tax payments (T)	Earnings after taxes[a] (Y)	Net cash flow to equity[b] (NCF)	Accounting rate of return to initial equity (%)
1	—	—	—	—	(10)	—
2	—	—	—	—	(10)	—
3	—	—	—	—	(10)	—
4	—	—	—	—	(10)	—
5	—	—	—	—	(10)	—
6	(16.6)	—	—	—	9.6	0.0
7	(26.4)	—	—	—	19.4	0.0
8	(26.8)	—	—	—	19.8	0.0
9	(27.2)	—	—	—	20.2	0.0
10	(3.0)	24.6	12.3	12.3	8.3	24.6
11	—	28.0	14.0	14.0	7.0	28.0
12	—	28.4	14.2	14.2	7.2	28.4
13	—	28.8	14.4	14.4	7.4	28.8
14	—	29.2	14.6	14.6	7.6	29.2
15	—	29.6	14.8	14.8	7.8	29.5
16	—	30.0	15.0	15.0	13.0	30.0
17	—	30.0	15.0	15.0	13.0	30.0
18	—	30.0	15.0	15.0	13.0	30.0
19	—	30.0	15.0	15.0	13.0	30.0
20	—	30.0	15.0	15.0	13.0	30.0

Notes: Numbers in parentheses designate cash outflow in millions of dollars.
Internal rate of return to initial equity equals 16.6 percent.
Mean accounting rate of return to initial equity equals 21.2 percent.
[a] Assumes 50 percent tax on taxable income (TI):
$$TI = R - C - I - D$$
$$Y = TI - T$$
where $T =$ tax payments.
[b] $NCF = R - C - I - T - L - CE$. During the first five years NCF represents
equity outflow.

depreciation method used in the preparation of the tax return differs
from the method used in reports to stockholders in the same year.
When accelerated depreciation allowances are exhausted, the accumulated deferred tax is drawn on to compensate for the excess of tax
liabilities over what they would have been had accelerated depreciation not been available. The philosophy behind this is that a company
should not obtain higher profits in earlier years during a full
depreciation write-off at the expense of profits in later years when
depreciation for tax purposes has been fully utilized. Under such an
accounting procedure, the purpose of accelerated depreciation is not
to pay higher dividends but rather to assure the company of a
sufficiently large cash flow during the early years to meet debt service

and to build up cash reserves which could be used either for debt service payments or for higher dividends later on.

Amortization and Depletion. Two other types of capital consumption allowances should be mentioned, namely, amortization and depletion. Although, in the example given in Tables 2 and 3, it was assumed that all initial capital expenditures consisted of investment in depreciable assets, some capitalized expenditures such as geological and exploration costs and mine preparation expense do not involve the acquisition of a physical capital asset subject to depreciation. Nevertheless, a certain proportion of these capitalized expenditures should be charged as an indirect expense each year until they have been fully amortized. The capital value of these expenditures declines as the ore body is depleted so that amortization charges reflect capital consumption. Most mine development agreements or general mining or tax laws provide for amortization of such capitalized expenditures over the period of the contract or in accordance with some formula.

The original purpose of depletion as an annual charge against gross operating income for determining taxable income was to recognize the erosion of the value of the mining or petroleum properties arising from the exhaustion of the resources. However, this purpose has come to be confused with a second purpose, that of providing an incentive to exploration and investment in mining and petroleum. There are two basic methods of depletion, mainly, *cost depletion* and *percentage depletion.*[6] Cost depletion is analogous to depreciation, in that it is calculated with reference to the cost of the property and the annual amounts of minerals yielded by the property. Thus if a mine contains an estimated 20 million tons of ore and the cost of the property is $10 million, under cost depletion in the first year of operation depletion would be charged at the rate of 50 cents per ton, or a total of $100,000, if 200,000 tons were produced.

Under percentage depletion, depletion can be charged without reference to the cost basis (as in the case of cost depletion), and if a property has a large ore body with reserves to permit operations, say, for fifty years, cumulative depletion at the rate of 15 percent of gross

[6] Under U.S. tax law, taxpayers may compute the depletion allowance on either the cost depletion or the percentage depletion basis, using the higher figure. Under the percentage depletion method, a flat percentage of gross income from the property is allowable as a depletion deduction subject to a limitation of 50 percent of the net taxable income from the property. The rates to be applied to gross income from the property depend upon the mineral involved. Such rates range from a low of 5 percent for gravel, sand, and certain types of stone and clay up to a high of 22 percent for oil and gas and a broad list of metallic minerals.

income (limited to 50 percent of net income) may in time well exceed the cost of the property. Hence, percentage depletion is usually regarded more as an incentive to investment than an allowance of capital consumption.

In recent years, the depletion allowance has become outmoded both in general mining laws of developing countries and in mine development contracts. As will be noted in the case study on Toquepala, the Peruvian government substantially reduced the depletion allowance and made it available only when reinvested. This occurred after the Toquepala mine went into operation. Depletion has been severely criticized in some developing countries on grounds that it constitutes a charge for the value of minerals in the ground, which are regarded as the property of the state and not of the private enterprise exploiting them. However, this criticism misses the point. Minerals have no value in the ground, especially if no one knows whether they exist in commercial quantities. Companies acquire rights to explore for and to exploit minerals, often by payments for concessions and/or payments for the land, and they expend large sums for exploration and development. The capitalized value of these outlays depends ultimately on the ability of the property to yield a net revenue, which in turn depends upon the mineral resources in the ground and the prices for which the refined minerals may be sold in the marketplace. A more serious criticism is that in cases where depreciation and amortization are provided for, depletion constitutes a duplicate capital consumption allowance. One might argue, however, that depletion should apply to the capitalized value of a mine, that is, the present value of expected net returns, over and above the actual capital outlays to which depreciation and amortization apply under the tax arrangements. However, developing countries have generally refused to recognize such capitalized value as appropriate for a capital consumption allowance. It still might be argued that depletion is useful as an incentive, but there may be other incentives which are more attractive to investors, while at the same time less costly in terms of tax revenues to the host country.

In some countries the mining laws do not provide for depreciation, amortization, or depletion allowances. This is true, for example, in Zambia, where mining companies are allowed to write off capital expenditures in the year in which they occur, and new mines pay no profits taxes until the original capitalization and subsequent capital expenditures have been recovered. In the case of existing mines in Zambia, the balance of the unredeemed capital expenditures outstanding on April 1, 1970, may be written off in equal installments over twenty years or over the life of the mine, whichever is shorter. No depletion allowances are permitted. Doubtless there are advantages and disadvantages for foreign mining enterprises arising from both systems of taxation.

TECHNICAL AND ECONOMIC FACTORS IN CASH FLOW ANALYSIS

Cash flow analysis for mine projects must be based on a great deal of geological, engineering, metallurgical, construction, transportation, and other infrastructure information, which cannot be described adequately within this study. However, for an analysis of the profitability of a mine, it is important to note the general areas of uncertainty in the generation of the basic engineering data. Fundamental to the estimates of both capital expenditures and direct operating costs are the surveying and metallurgical testing of the ore body. Since the grade of the ore varies substantially over the ore body, the more extensive the drilling and testing, the more accurate the data on which to determine capital and operating costs. But such information requires both time and capital outlays, so there is a tradeoff between the value of additional information for the reliability of the cash flow analysis on the one hand, and the additional cost of obtaining such information on the other. Where investors operate under general mining laws that establish the tax and other conditions of exploitation without the necessity of negotiating special contracts with the government, mining firms carry on exploration and evaluation activities up to the point at which they have sufficient information to determine the profitability of the mine project under the conditions established by existing legislation. But today in most developing countries it is necessary to negotiate specific mine development contracts whose terms may vary with the economic evaluation of the project. Since the contract terms demanded by the host government may prove unacceptable to the investor, mining firms are reluctant to make outlays which may run from $10–$15 million beyond those required for a preliminary evaluation of the mine without first negotiating a contract. On the other hand, successful contract negotiation often requires more precise cost estimates than can be made on the basis of the preliminary evaluation. For the investor, the larger the degree of uncertainty, the higher will be the expected rate of return necessary to justify the investment. But the host country may be reluctant to agree to terms that might give the government a relatively small share of the earnings. Referring again to Kennecott's Ok Tedi project, the contract negotiations with the government were stalled for many months, in part because the PNG government was insisting that the company undertake more drilling and mine evaluation, while Kennecott refused to make additional capital outlays without a contract.[7]

Even where the grade of the ore body is well established, capital outlays for mining and metallurgical equipment and infrastructure made over a four- to five-year period are subject to a considerable margin of error, perhaps 15 percent or more. There are nearly always unforeseen contingencies involving cost overruns, especially since each mine is unique. Where a mine is located in an isolated mountain or jungle region in the developing country, it is frequently not possible to draw on the experience of other mines located in identical environments. In cases where half or more of the investment is financed by borrowing, debt service during the first decade of operation may exceed operating costs. Assuming constant prices of the inputs, operating costs can usually be estimated with reasonable accuracy once the grade of ore and technical processes to be used are established; the greatest uncertainty arises from the estimation of wages and material inputs. Wages usually account for about 40 percent of direct operating costs, and in recent years wage and fringe benefits have been highly volatile. Even more serious are strikes that impair revenue, since fixed costs, including debt service, tend to exceed variable costs. In Peru, Cerro de Pasco has in some years lost more than 15 percent of its output as a consequence of strikes. In some countries, such as Zaire and Zambia, work stoppages are rare, while in Chile and Peru they have been a major factor in revenue fluctuation. Neither government ownership of the mines, as in Chile, nor a military government, as in Peru, has proved a barrier to substantial losses of production from strikes. Moreover, in most developing countries, the government loses more revenue from work stoppages than do the private investors.

Fixed capital outlays, other than normal replacement, continue after production is initiated. Additional mine development and infrastructure are required nearly every year, and additional mill and hauling equipment are usually needed in order to maintain output as the ore grade declines. For example, at the Bougainville mine in PNG, a new ball mill was added during the second year of production, and, if output is to be maintained, additional ball mills must be provided

---

[7] Mikesell, *Foreign Investment in Copper Mining in Papua New Guinea.*

every year or so as the average grade of the ore mined declines from 0.75 percent to less than 0.5 percent over the next decade. Therefore, the ability to anticipate further fixed capital expenditures depends in part on the accuracy of the evaluation of the ore body.

Price Projections

Far greater uncertainty is involved in the estimation of the prices of mine products over the operating life of the mine. Since we are concerned here with decisions to invest in new mines requiring four or five years to construct, the relevant price variable in the decision is a range of expected prices over a ten- to twenty-year period, beginning several years after the initiation of construction. Moreover, the relevant price variable is the constant or relative long-run price, since few decision makers care to project the general trend of world prices.[8] The projection period is long enough to cover several normal recessions, the timing of which could not be projected. In recent years, statisticians and econometricians have formulated models for projecting the price of copper and other metals, but whatever value they have decreases rapidly with the time period, and by their very nature the models are not suitable for long-run forecasting.[9] Price expectations as such are frequently less important in investment decisions than long-run, world demand projections in relation to projections of world mine capacity. Another common criterion is the relationship of expected production costs for the mine in question to the pattern of per unit costs in existing mines and to cost trends throughout the world. Such analysis provides a basis for judgments with regard to minimum and maximum long-run average prices. Given the expected rate of growth in demand for the product, costs tend to set a floor on prices in the intermediate run, since new investment in existing mines for increasing or maintaining output is not likely to take place if the cost–price ratio

[8] A decline in the general price level, even with no decline in the relative price of the product, would mean a relative rise in the value of fixed debt service. However, in recent years a substantial or sustained decline in the general level of world prices has been almost unthinkable.

[9] A good example of an econometric forecasting model is provided by F. M. Fisher, P. H. Cootner, and M. N. Baily in "An Econometric Model of the World Copper Industry," *The Bell Journal of Economics and Management Science* (Autumn 1972), p. 568–609. Regarding their own projections, the authors state, "The first thing to note about these forecasts is that they are undoubtedly better as one-year projections than as forecasts over several years" [pp. 598–599]. Thus, their forecasts of the LME price of copper for 1969, using 1968 exogenous data, are quite good, but for the years beyond 1969, at least through 1973, their forecasts are quite wide of the mark.

rises above a certain point.[10] Likewise, costs for new mines in the lower-cost producing areas tend to set a ceiling on the long-run average price of the product. Of course, projections of price ranges can be upset by large new discoveries of high-grade deposits or by new technological developments such as that which led to relatively low-cost production of low-grade ores in large open-pit mines.

Mining firms do not rely on their own price projections alone. Research organizations, such as the Stanford Research Institute, and the research departments of large banks, such as the Chase Manhattan Bank, are continually making projections, and at any given point there develops a kind of concensus regarding the long-run outlook. This long-run price outlook is constantly being adjusted by changes in planned capacity. A number of five- and six-year projections of planned new mine capacity in copper exist, most of them based on the same data. Since worldwide banking consortia, together with government export credit institutions, such as the Export–Import Bank of Washington, provide a substantial amount of capital for new mines in the developing countries, the long-run price projections of the financial community take on special significance.

An element in future price uncertainty is the possibility that one or more large importing countries will impose duties on imports of the product or duties that discriminate against imports from the country in which the mine is located. Throughout much of the period following World War II, the United States imposed protective import duties on copper, which had the effect of lowering prices to producers outside the United States. The United States also imposed price ceilings on copper products, which had the effect of reducing the demand for high-priced foreign copper, even though domestic output was insufficient to satisfy domestic demand.

Forward Contracts and Sales to Affiliates

Investors often negotiate long-term contracts with smelters or refineries in other countries, with the contracts running for ten to fifteen years, usually well beyond the period of debt repayment. In recent years, the contracts have usually provided for sales at prices governed by the LME price. In some contracts, as is the case with those of the Bougainville mine, there is a guaranteed minimum price. When the

---

[10] For a discussion of the views of mining officials on long-run prices in relation to production costs, see Orris C. Herfindahl, *Copper Costs and Prices: 1870–1957* (Baltimore: Johns Hopkins University Press for Resources for the Future, 1959), pp. 147–152.

LME price is below the guaranteed minimum, the purchaser is given a credit in an amount equal to the difference between the LME price and the minimum price at which the product is sold. In the 1960s long-term contracts were usually only available for concentrates. The negotiation of such contracts may preclude the establishment of processing facilities in the ore-producing country. The ability to negotiate long-term contracts for concentrates with Japan and Germany was an important factor in the decision to invest in the Bougainville mine.

When the investing company has downstream affiliates, it may have an assured market for all or a large proportion of its output of concentrates or blister or even for refined copper. Joint ventures involving several integrated firms may also provide an assured market for the products of a mine. Thus, in the case of the Toquepala mine, a substantial proportion of the output is sold to the four U.S. companies having an equity interest in the SPCC.

THE MINIMUM EXPECTED RATE OF RETURN

Most mining companies have adopted the minimum expected rate of return necessary to induce them to make an investment, but this criterion is not rigid since the actual investment decision is determined by a complex of interrelated factors unique to each decision. Capital expenditures, production costs, debt service, projected product prices, and other variables that go into cash flow analysis yield an expected rate of return in which the investor can have confidence only to the degree of the reliability of each of the many inputs. It is possible to make subjective estimates of the probability distribution of each input variable in the cash flow and rate-of-return calculation. By means of probability analysis and the employment of the Monte Carlo model, or a similar approach, it is possible to calculate the rate of return at the 95 percent or 90 percent lower and upper confidence limits.[11] Most mining firms do not employ a scientific model involving the probability distribution for each of the input variables, but they usually calculate cash flow for a range of projected product prices and frequently for a range of capital expenditures and operating costs. Such calculations provide the basis for a crude determination of the rate of return

[11] See Brian W. Mackenzie, "Evaluating the Economics of Mine Development," Part I, *Canadian Mining Journal* (December 1970), pp. 40–47; and Part II (March 1971), pp. 46–54. See also, David B. Hertz, "Risk Analysis and Capital Investment," *Harvard Business Review* (January/February 1964), pp. 95–106.

corresponding to the lower confidence limit at, say, the 95 percent confidence level. This calculation is likely to play a crucial role in the negotiations with the host government on the tax regime, including accelerated depreciation and tax holidays, even though the most probable rate of return may be more important to the investment decision, provided satisfactory tax and other conditions can be negotiated. The rate of return corresponding to the lower confidence limit must ordinarily be high enough for the firm to meet payments on the loans and, therefore, may be the determining factor in the supply of loans and credits. Thus we are dealing with two critical expected rates of return—the most probable expected rate and the rate of return at the lower confidence limit.

Some investment prospects may be characterized by a high probable rate of return accompanied by a very low rate of return corresponding to the lower confidence limit, while others may involve a more modest probable rate of return but a smaller differential between the probable rate of return and that corresponding to the lower confidence limit. Whether a mining firm opts for a more profitable but more risky investment—assuming it has a choice—depends upon company preference and also upon the composition of its portfolio. A large company with a well-diversified portfolio might well be more inclined to make an investment in a project which entails considerable risk but with the expectation of high profits, while a less-diversified firm might reject such a project.

POLITICAL RISKS

The type of risks that we have been discussing represents the normal economic risks peculiar to the mining industry, and the success of a mining firm greatly depends upon the experience and ability of its management and professional staff in dealing with such risks. However, there is another class of risk, namely, the political risk of expropriation, of contract violations by the host government, or of war and civil disturbance, for which there is no actuarial information, and the ability and experience of the firm can play little or no role in determining the probability distribution of the events. The recent history of a country with respect to its treatment of foreign investors provides some guide in assessing risks, as do the general policies of the government in power. But the greatest risk comes from a revolutionary change (not necessarily violent revolution) involving the coming to power of a government adhering to policies quite antithetical to foreign investors.

Even governments that have been favorable to foreign investment may change their policies as a consequence of pressure from a strong opposition party that threatens to win the next election over the issue of national ownership or control of resource industries.[12] If the history of the country is such that companies have no confidence in contractual arrangements made by the government, foreign firms are unlikely to be willing to make investments or to carry out exploration activities, even if potential returns on an economic basis are very large. When the political situation is moderately risky in the longer run but relatively secure in the intermediate run, a company may insist on a level of after-tax profits that will enable it to achieve an acceptable internal rate of return calculated, not over the expected life of the mine of, say, fifteen or twenty years, but over a shorter period, say, six or eight years, after the initiation of commercial production. For a given internal rate of return, the annual volume of earnings must be higher the shorter the period over which the return is calculated.[13]

An important risk in the minds of foreign investors is that arising from the possibility that the investor may not be able to convert revenues into foreign exchange for payment of debt obligations or dividends, or for the purchase of imports required to operate a mining project. This risk occurs in countries where the minerals are sold largely to domestic firms, or where the host government requires that all foreign exchange earnings be surrendered to the central bank. Frequently, potential foreign lenders to the mining enterprise will refuse to make loans unless an amount of the foreign exchange revenues sufficient to meet the debt obligations (plus any cash reserve that may be required under the credit agreement) is retained abroad. In some cases the potential investor may insist on retaining all or a portion of the foreign exchange earnings abroad in order to ensure the availability of foreign exchange for dividend payments and for imports of goods and services required by the mining enterprise. This

[12] A good example is provided by the 1969 action of President Eduardo Frei of Chile, who demanded 51 percent ownership of Anaconda's properties just three years after an agreement had been made with Anaconda for a large expansion of its copper mining capacity in Chile. This action was undoubtedly influenced by the political campaign of Sen. Salvador Allende, who was advocating complete nationalization of all large foreign mining enterprises.

[13] In the calculation of internal rates of return, the period of cash inflow may be the estimated life of the mine or the length of the mining contract, or it may be an arbitrarily chosen short period. In some cases, an amount equal to the estimated liquidation value of the mine is added to cash inflow for the last year. This is usually not more than net current assets, since fixed assets in a mine are likely to have little value except in the mine as a going concern. For any estimated stream of NCF, the internal rate of return tends to rise with the time period over which it is calculated, eventually approaching a limit after about twenty years.

may prove to be a serious problem for a country whose laws or regulations require the repatriation of all foreign exchange earnings. Sometimes the issue can be resolved by the establishment of a special account in a foreign bank in the name of the finance ministry but subject to special conditions regarding withdrawals of the funds. Such an arrangement was provided in the bilateral agreement between the SPCC and the Peruvian government for the development of the Cuajone mine.

It is possible for large companies to reduce the incidence of political risk by investing in a number of developing countries, much in the same way that an international security investor seeks to reduce his risks by including in his portfolio the securities of a number of countries. Sound portfolio practice involves tradeoffs between risk and the level of returns, so that investors will normally require higher returns on investments in countries regarded as presenting a higher degree of risk. Spreading risk over a number of countries undoubtedly provides an advantage to large mining companies over smaller companies that can invest in only one or two areas. However, the capital outlay requirements for a copper mining project have increased from $25 million or less three decades ago to several hundred million dollars, the current sum required for low-grade ore, open-pit mines. This increase in capital outlay has rendered the risk exposure in supplying the bulk of the capital in the form of equity investment too great for even the largest mining companies. This helps to explain why most large mining ventures today are financed heavily by loans and credits obtained from a broad list of sources. Foreign investment insurance by the Overseas Private Investment Corporation (OPIC) and by similar governmental agencies in other developed countries has frequently been an essential condition for investment in the extractive industries.

OTHER FACTORS IN INVESTMENT DECISIONS

The expected rate of return with due allowance for risk is by no means the only factor in mining industry investment decisions. Firms will often prefer an investment in one geographic area or country over another in order to diversify their assets or their sources of supply for a commodity. One firm may be willing to negotiate a mine development contract under terms that would be unacceptable to another because the first firm is more anxious to expand its operations or to replace output lost by the exhaustion of a mine or by expropriation.[14] Most large mining firms carry out geological surveys and explorations in many areas of the world and endeavor to develop an inventory of potential projects.[15]

If it is an integrated firm, the decision to make an investment may depend heavily on the firm's need for sources of supply for its affiliates. It may also depend upon the degree to which the resources of the firm are being utilized. The resources of a large mining firm are not simply the funds it has available for equity investment or what it can borrow. At any given time, a firm is limited by its managerial and technical personnel as to the number of projects it can take on. On the other hand, the resources of the firm may be underemployed, in which case it may be anxious to undertake new ventures and hence accept a somewhat lower rate of return. Finally, there appears to be an imitative pattern among mining firms. When one firm goes into a country or geographic area, others may follow, with the followers often willing to contract on somewhat less favorable terms than the leader. This is well illustrated by the widespread movement of mining firms to Indonesia. Following the 1967 investment of Freeport Indonesia in the Ertsberg copper project, shortly after the overthrow of the Sukarno government, a number of firms became interested in obtaining mining concessions in that country.

METHODS OF FINANCING

The expected rate of return to the investor is greatly affected by the method of financing. For a given project, the higher the loan–equity ratio, the higher the expected rate of return to equity will normally be. This is true because the interest rate on borrowed capital will

---

[14] I was told by an executive of a mining firm operating in a developed country that even though a further expansion of the firm's principal mine in the developed country afforded the greatest prospect for profitable investment, it was unlikely to make an additional investment in the near future because the company believed it should diversify geographically, both within the country and in other countries.

[15] In the past mining companies were permitted to maintain large concessions in developing countries for many years by the payment of a small fee. However, in recent years many developing countries have placed strict limits on how long un-worked concessions may be held. On August 14, 1970, the Peruvian government ordered all concession holders to present "critical path method-planned projects" for their concessions by September 30, 1970, which would then be reviewed by the government before acceptance. Following acceptance the companies were given until December 31, 1970, to arrange financing of the projects and to present proof of the availability of such financing. The time period for submitting plans was so short that virtually all of the large unworked concessions reverted to the state.

usually be less than the expected rate of return on equity that is necessary to attract the foreign investor. The rate of return to equity will also be higher, the longer the maturity of the loans. Many companies borrow in the international capital market in addition to obtaining supplier credits for the purchase of equipment. Since interest is regarded as a cost, it is to the advantage of both the foreign investor and the host government to obtain the lowest possible rates of interest. However, if loan capital should be provided by the foreign investor or an affiliate, it might be advantageous for the company to charge a high rate of interest, since this could be a way of obtaining earnings at a lower tax rate, or in excess of permitted profit transfers in cases where such transfers are limited. Because interest is a cost deductible from revenue in calculating taxable income, the rate of interest should be in line with those existing within the international money market. It should be said that in the case of most long-term loans made by bank consortia or other financing institutions, the rate of interest varies from period to period over the life of the loan, usually with the Eurodollar rate if it is a dollar loan.

In financing a mine project there are usually large infrastructure expenditures for roads, the creation of facilities for mining towns, and for power and communications that are not directly concerned with mine operations but are necessary for the establishment of the industry. Some, or all, of these outlays may be made by the foreign investor, or a portion may be made by the host government. This is an important part of the negotiations, but there are tradeoffs that the host government needs to keep in mind. For example, if the host government can borrow, say, from the World Bank, funds for the infrastructure required by a mining community at a lower rate of interest and for a longer term than they can be obtained by the foreign investor, taxable income—and hence tax revenues—will be higher if the host government provides the infrastructure. In fact, the additional tax revenue might well exceed by a substantial margin the annual debt service payments on the loan. This is true because if the company borrows the funds, interest payments and capital consumption allowances will be larger, both of which are deducted from revenues in the calculation of taxable income. Moreover, if the capital expenditures by the government are a substitute for equity investment, the host government would be in a position to demand a higher tax rate or perhaps a portion of the equity without cost. On the other hand, it might be argued that the host country should save its borrowing capacity from international loan agencies for financing other projects in the public sector.

Equity financing by the host government is often a controversial issue because of its relationship to control. However, I want to consider this question solely from the standpoint of the financial interest of the host country. Assume that a contract requires the foreign investor to sell 20 percent of the equity to the host government after the construction period. If the price paid for the equity shares is, say, 20 percent of the aggregate capital expenditures, the foreign investor will require a larger expected rate of return to compensate him for the return on the 20 percent equity investment for which he has received no return during the exploration and construction periods. Also, the foreign investor bears the risk on the 20 percent investment, since the host government will not take up the option unless the indicated return after the mine has gone into production is higher than the social rate of discount on capital for the host country.

The point here is that obtaining a portion of the equity either at book value or gratis may not be without cost. This is true even if the host country is permitted to pay for the equity out of dividends on the equity shares it receives. Indeed, the host country might have been financially better off, say, with a higher tax rate, or with the elimination of a tax holiday or of accelerated depreciation than with the acquisition of a portion of the equity. Somewhat different is the case where the host country forms a joint venture with the foreign investor from the beginning, sharing with the latter, say, on a 50–50 basis, all of the risk capital, including exploration, evaluation, and equity financing of construction. In contemplating a joint venture, the host government should compare the potential return from alternative uses of its capital with the expected additional returns from joint ownership over the expected tax revenues with 100 percent foreign ownership. In addition, in the case of joint ventures the foreign company, as a condition for its participation in the joint venture, usually demands a management contract and a management fee, which may run as high as 5 percent of the gross revenue. This could greatly reduce the returns to the host country.

Frequently, provision is made in contracts for the sale of equity to the public in the host country. Some companies favor this practice because it stimulates the local community's interest in the welfare of the equity holders. This type of financing creates problems since it is usually not possible to sell shares to the local public until earnings are well established. Even though the shares are sold at a substantial premium above the initial par value, the requirement to sell the shares may affect the foreign investor's expected rate of return and, hence, lead the company to demand compensatory concessions from the government at the time of the contract negotiations.

The Trend Toward High Debt–Equity Ratios

The financing of the Bougainville, Toquepala, and Cuajone mines, described in Part II, are examples of the modern trend toward high debt–equity ratios in the financing of large-scale mines with construction costs running into hundreds of millions of dollars. Large open-pit mines require a capital investment of $4,000 or more per annual ton of metal, and the profitable scale of operation runs from 50,000 to 200,000 tons per year. Thus mines costing $500 million or more are becoming common. Such a level of capital expenditures is well beyond the resources of the largest mining enterprises. In fact, two or three such mines exceed the net worth of most of the largest international mining enterprises. Predevelopment costs of large mines are running up to $30 million or more, and mining enterprises are tending to limit their equity contribution to the capitalized value of their predevelopment expenditures made over a period of five years or more. Because of the high risks involved in foreign mining ventures, mining enterprises are seeking an internal rate of return of at least 20 percent on their equity investment over a period of fifteen years or less. This would not be feasible at current tax rates without a substantial amount of leverage in the form of a high debt–equity ratio. This means that the bulk of the capital for the development of new large-scale mines— at least in developing countries—must come from the international capital market, and in recent years most of this capital has been provided by international consortia of commercial banks plus substantial suppliers' credits, which, in turn, may either be guaranteed by or financed by government lending agencies in the developed countries such as the Export–Import Bank. If these sources of international capital should no longer be available in the large amounts required for financing an expansion of the world's mineral industries, the capital would have to be supplied by institutions such as the World Bank, or the expansion of mineral industries in the developing countries would be greatly curtailed.

NEGOTIATING THE CONTRACT TERMS

In negotiating the mine contract, the major objectives of the prospective investor are (1) to maximize GCF during the period of debt repayment; (2) to maximize the expected internal rate of return to equity over the life of the mine or of the contract; (3) to assure complete freedom for management, production, marketing, and financial operations; and (4) to safeguard against changes in the conditions set forth in the contract or in the laws relating to the mining company's activities at the time the contract is signed.

The objectives of the government of the host country are (1) to maximize its income from mining operations and, in particular, to maximize the government's share of net earnings; (2) to avoid relinquishing any rights to control over company policies and operations such as marketing, hiring, and foreign exchange; and (3) to maximize the contribution of the mine operations to the economic welfare and development of the host country through the purchase of local goods and services, labor training, and the provision of infrastructure and social services.

At the time of the contract negotiations, the bargaining position of the company is at a maximum. The company has the information obtained through years of exploration and evaluation and is prepared to go ahead with the proposed mine project, provided a satisfactory contract can be negotiated. The host government is anxious to have the investment made since it promises to yield millions of dollars in foreign exchange income and thousands of jobs, and to provide a stimulus to local business. Host governments must depend very largely on the company for information regarding the project, although the government may hire an independent firm to review the feasibility study prepared by the mining company. Ideally, the tax and other conditions affecting the division of the rents between the mining company and the host government should be determined by international competitive bidding on projects for which feasibility studies have been prepared. However, most developing countries must depend on international mining companies to undertake the exploration and evaluation of projects, since this requires high-risk capital with odds for success on the order of ten to one. Large international companies can afford to undertake such risks with the expectation that if only one out of ten exploration projects proves profitable, they will earn enough on the one to cover the exploration costs of the remaining nine. Such diversification over a wide geographic area is usually not possible for developing countries.[16] Should negotiations break down, the company will probably lose its exploration concession, but it would require

[16] The UN Economic and Social Council has recently established a Revolving Fund to assist developing countries in the exploration of mineral, water, and energy resources. The successful operation of this fund might alter the bargaining conditions in negotiations with foreign private firms for the development of mineral resources.

several years before another company would undertake the necessary exploration and evaluation for negotiating a contract. Moreover, the fact that negotiations broke down with the first company might well discourage another company from investing several million dollars preparatory to negotiating a contract.

At the beginning of negotiations, both the company and the host government are likely to be guided to some extent by the mine contracts in the same industry that have been negotiated by the same or other developing countries in recent years. Thus, most contracts today provide for a tax on net earnings of 40–50 percent, a royalty ranging from 1–2 percent of the gross value of output, and frequently include some provision for equity participation by the host government. Renegotiated contracts for mines that have been producing for twenty years or longer are much more favorable to the host government than are the more recent contracts. For example, the Zambian contracts negotiated in 1969 provide for the tax on net earnings of 73 percent, with 51 percent of the equity to be sold to the Zambian government. Such an arrangement is unlikely to be attractive to companies negotiating a contract for a new mining venture.

An examination of existing mine development contracts of recent vintage reveals a bewildering combination of terms covering tax and royalty rates, tax holidays, depreciation schedules, loan–equity ratios, government and local public participation, government provision for infrastructure, import duties, land fees and rentals, and other conditions. The broad variety of these conditions is illustrated in Appendix B, which provides a summary of the contract terms for three mining agreements. The varying combinations of terms make it exceedingly difficult to compare contracts on the basis of their relative overall advantage to the host country. The rate of return to the foreign investor will depend not simply upon the contract terms, but upon the grade of the ore, the metallurgy, cost of transportation, the capital–output ratio, and other technical factors. Also, the effects of the same contract provisions with respect to taxation, royalties, depreciation, and government equity participation will have greatly differing effects on the distribution of before-tax revenue between the company and the host government, depending upon the level of revenues over time and the method of financing the project; for example, the ratio of loan to equity financing.

An alternative approach in mine contract negotiations is for both the company and the officials of the host government to prepare a cash flow analysis based on the technical data derived from the project evaluation and then to calculate the returns to both the company and the government on the basis of varying contract provisions and methods of financing. If the government is interested in comparing the effects of a specific set of terms with those contained in existing contracts involving other countries and companies, it can then apply the tax and other provisions in the contracts negotiated in other countries to the cash flow projections for the project in question. This is a much more accurate way of determining whether the provisions negotiated in other contracts are more or less favorable to the government than those it may be considering. The negotiating parties may find that the cash flow projections which each party has prepared, perhaps based on differing projections of product prices and other factors, may differ between them, but these differences can usually be resolved on a technical basis.

Once agreement has been reached on the cash flow projections before allowance for taxes, there is ordinarily a range of expected rates of return within which bargaining can take place. The company will have in mind a minimum expected rate of return to equity below which it will not go, and if there is large debt financing, the company —as well as the prospective creditors—will usually insist on low or zero taxes during all or a portion of the period of the debt repayment. Of course, no company is going to reveal the price below which it will never invest, thereby surrendering an exploration concession on which it may have already spent millions of dollars. Therefore, it is important for the host government to have knowledge of the limits within which successful bargaining can take place. For example, few if any companies today are likely to agree to a 12 percent internal rate of return, while most companies would not turn down an opportunity for a 20 percent return. Within this range companies will be influenced by such considerations as their desire to control a larger share of the world's mine capacity, their evaluation of the economic and political risks, or by the other factors discussed above.

For a foreign investor to demand a very high rate of return (with little left for the host government) because of high political risk might prove to be counterproductive. If such a contract were negotiated, the existence of a high rate of return might well encourage an expropriation or a demand for renegotiation. Nevertheless, host countries will be in a far better bargaining position over conditions affecting the expected rate of return if they take steps that reduce potential risks in the minds of foreign investors. Such steps might include adopting legislation to enable the foreign company to obtain investment insurance, such as that provided by the OPIC, and agreeing to a provision in the contract for international arbitration of disputes by the

International Center for Settlement of Investment Disputes (ICSID) or a similar international tribunal.

The prospective rate of return on a foreign mineral investment may also entail a risk for the host government. If returns are exceptionally high relative to the minimum rate of return necessary to attract the foreign investor, and if the contract is written for a long period, say, twenty or thirty years, there will be widespread dissatisfaction with the agreement, criticism of the government officials who negotiated it, and a demand—often by the leaders of an opposing political party— to repudiate the agreement. This puts the government in a dilemma. On the one hand it feels it is not receiving a fair share of the rents from its mineral resources, yet it is reluctant to impair its investment climate by demanding a renegotiation of an agreement made in good faith by both parties.

This situation, which has occurred all too frequently in the past, suggests that contracts might be written so as to provide for a sharing of the before-tax revenues more favorable to the government if after a period of, say, ten years, the foreign investor has enjoyed a return substantially in excess of the minimum rate of return that made the original investment attractive. It is important that these conditions be fully specified in the contract. I believe it is equally important that host countries do not demand all or nearly all of the revenues beyond a certain rate of return to the foreign investor, since this will affect the willingness of the foreign investor to reinvest profits and to maximize the productivity of the mine. A good rule to follow might be to establish those conditions in a contract under which it will always be in the interest of both the foreign investor and the host country to maximize before-tax revenues over time. A corollary of this rule is that any conflicts that arise should be subject to what I have called joint maximizing solutions, that is, those that do not increase the share of one party at the expense of the total revenue pie.[17]

Once a division of the rents over time has been agreed upon, the mix of contract provisions can be negotiated from the standpoint of convenience and the objectives of the parties. For example, if it is politically important for the host government to acquire a share of the equity, this can usually be worked out—again, subject to the minimum

---

[17] For a discussion of conflicts between host governments and foreign investors in the resource industries, see Raymond F. Mikesell, "Conflict in Foreign Investor–Host Country Relations: A Preliminary Analysis," in *Foreign Investment in the Petroleum and Mineral Industries: Case Studies of Investor–Host Country Relations* (Baltimore: Johns Hopkins University Press for Resources for the Future, 1971), pp. 29–55.

expected rate of return necessary to induce the foreign investment. As has been noted, there may be cases in which it is advantageous for the host government to provide a substantial share of the infrastructure related to the mining project. Again, there may be cases in which the suppliers of loan capital to the mining venture will require a rapid accumulation of cash reserves through accelerated depreciation or by other means. High initial rates of return demanded by the suppliers of equity capital can be compensated by higher taxes in later periods adjusted to the rate of profit. On the other hand, the host government may have an urgent need for income in the short run; this could be balanced against a somewhat higher return for the foreign investor in the longer run. Also, provisions may be added to the contract that reduce the foreign investor's tax obligations in his home country. Moreover, the host country may want to keep in mind that the U.S. foreign investor receives a tax credit, up to the amount of his U.S. tax liability, against income taxes paid abroad. Hence, taxes levied by the host government up to that amount do not constitute a burden on the company. On the other hand, the company cannot offset royalties against its U.S. tax liabilities; royalties are treated like any other cost and deducted from gross revenue. Thus, in a manner which contributes to the convenience of the negotiating parties, the varying options in the contract terms can be used to realize an agreed minimum rate of return to the foreign investor and a sharing of the rents above that minimum rate of return. This approach appears to have advantages over trying to pattern each provision on some international standard.

LIVING UNDER A MINE DEVELOPMENT AGREEMENT

The record for maintaining mine development agreements in recent years has been notably poor. Aside from honest disputes regarding the legal interpretation of contract provisions, host governments frequently demand a renegotiation of terms, threatening expropriation if the company does not comply. There have also been a number of cases of expropriation or demands that the company yield majority equity interest to the government with compensation based on terms largely dictated by the host government. Complete expropriation, or the demand for majority equity ownership within the contract period, is a political act usually taken in response to an ideological or other non-economic motivation. Occasionally disputes over the legality or interpretation of a contract or dissatisfaction with the activities of the company have led governments to expropriation, but such occasions are rare. As a rule a government has more to gain economically by renegotiating the terms of the contract than by expropriation. Apart from ideological motivations, expropriation constitutes a "warfare solution" to a dispute from which both sides almost inevitably suffer economic losses. I shall, therefore, direct the following discussion to the economic factors leading to contract violation or to a demand for renegotiation.

Contracts are negotiated under conditions of uncertainty by both parties. As has already been mentioned, companies tend to calculate the minimum expected rate of return required for making an investment on the basis of the probability distribution of the relative variables in the calculation. It is not surprising therefore that in recent years, given the absence of serious depressions and continuously rising world prices, profitability has tended to exceed expectations, at least the expectations of the host government. Once the investment is made and the project proves profitable, the bargaining power of the host government is greatly enhanced, tempered only by its desire to maintain the image of a favorable climate for other investors. Inevitably the host government will be under strong pressures internally, as well as from the public and the opposition political parties, to seek a larger share of the rent. Unless constrained by the domestic courts, the government has the power to demand renegotiation of terms under the threat of expropriation.[18] It is generally accepted in international law that a government has the power to nationalize an industry no matter what agreements may have been made to the contrary with private parties. To the extent that it is relevant, international law applies only to the right of the foreign investor to adequate and prompt compensation. The company will usually prefer renegotiation to expropriation, since compensation is almost never adequate in terms of the "going concern" value. Even though a company might believe it could win its case against a government demanding renegotiation in the domestic courts or in an international tribunal (if one is provided for in the agreement), the ultimate sanction of expropriation remains with the government.[19]

---

[18] In some developing countries courts tend to follow the will of the government in power, especially when dealing with a foreign company. In any case, the independence of the courts is usually not as great as it is in the United States.

[19] Nationalization usually requires a specific act of the legislature, but such action will supersede any provision of an agreement.

Conflict and Relative Bargaining Strength

In an earlier study, I advanced the hypothesis of more or less continuous conflict between foreign investors in resource industries and the governments of host countries in developing countries, in the course of which the bargaining power of the foreign investor is always greatest before a new investment is made and lowest after a new investment project is completed and has proved profitable.[20] This rather obvious conclusion is well illustrated by the recent histories of the Bougainville and SPCC operations. In PNG there was a strong movement for renegotiating the contract with BCL within a year of the initiation of commercial operations beginning in April 1972. Partly as a consequence of extraordinarily large profits earned by BCL in 1973, a renegotiation was initiated on a government demand in early 1974, leading to a radical change in the tax regime and the division of the earnings generated by the enterprise in the new agreement reached in October 1974. It might be said, however, that the PNG government was somewhat restrained in its demands by the possibility of negotiating an agreement for the construction of another large copper mine which had been explored by Kennecott Copper Corporation, its negotiations having been delayed pending the renegotiation with BCL. Since it is likely that the tax conditions offered Kennecott will be similar to those negotiated with BCL in 1974, it will be interesting to see whether Kennecott or any other international company is willing to proceed with the construction of the mine on the same terms.

The SPCC's recent experience in Peru is perhaps even more illustrative of the operation of bargaining strategy. Since the inauguration of the Velasco Administration in 1969, the Peruvian government has expropriated several large foreign investments in the resource industries, including Exxon's International Petroleum Company and the large Cerro de Pasco mining complex formerly owned by the Cerro Corporation. Nearly all of the large undeveloped mining properties held by foreign enterprises were also expropriated. However, the Velasco Administration negotiated a mine development contract with the SPCC for the Cuajone copper mine, which was to cost over $500 million. For several years, work on the Cuajone mine has been financed out of cash flow generated by the Toquepala mine, pending the securing of large external loans and suppliers' credits totaling several

[20] Mikesell, "Conflict in Foreign Investor–Host Country Relations," pp. 29–55.

hundred million dollars for the completion of Cuajone. Meanwhile, the SPCC has been relatively free of harassment and threats of expropriation such as those which have been experienced by virtually all the other large, foreign-owned resource companies in Peru. Evidently the SPCC and its owners are betting that their usefulness to the host country will continue to be recognized and the scenario of expropriation or demand for radical renegotiation will not be repeated once Cuajone has been completed, or at least not until they have recovered their capital at a reasonable rate of return.

Can Conflict Be Reduced?

Much of the conflict and the breaking of agreements by host governments has an ideological basis, and governments that want to stay in power are often led by political pressure to actions which are not in the best interests of the country. As has been noted, however, there are economic bases for conflicts that arise from the uncertainties of the outcome of an investment before it is made. In addition, international standards with respect to the division of the before-tax earnings between foreign investors and the host country, as well as other contract conditions, tend to change over a period of several decades. Such changes in the international standards for new contracts inevitably lead governments that have negotiated mine agreements a decade or two in the past to demand renegotiation in order to bring their contracts into line with the terms of those currently being consummated.

Given the uncertainties regarding the profitability of mining operations several years in the future, a company may demand, as a condition for making an investment, a period of zero or low taxes covering the time during which it expects to repay its external indebtedness and recover its equity. But if initial earnings are unexpectedly large and a company is able to pay large dividends while enjoying freedom from taxation, the government will be under strong pressure to demand renegotiation. This is well illustrated by the experience of the Bougainville mine, which proved to be exceptionally profitable from the start, but the provision in the original contract that allowed a combination of a tax holiday followed by accelerated depreciation and a gradual increase in the tax rate to a somewhat modest level meant that the government would receive no corporate taxes for the first seven years of operations, and only a modest tax would be applied for several years thereafter. Consequently, some flexibility built into the original contract, or a provision for renegotiation after several years, might have mitigated or avoided the conflict and renegotiation in 1974. The renegotiation occurred during a period of very high copper prices, but by the time the negotiations had been completed in October 1974 the price of copper had fallen very sharply. The imposition of a 70 percent tax rate on all profits might have spelled severe financial difficulty for BCL in subsequent years, especially in the light of its large remaining indebtedness. Fortunately, the new agreement provided for a minimum tax of 33⅓ percent on profits up to A$86 million (or 15 percent of asset value plus increased investment), beyond which profits are to be taxed at the 70 percent rate.

As a means of reducing conflict it is suggested that provision might be made in mine development agreements for a review of contracts, say, every five years, following the period of full capital recoupment. If the past and projected NCF to equity holders (after allowance for debt payments and reinvested depreciation) exceeds an agreed minimum internal rate of return over the life of the contract, an additional tax might be imposed. (Likewise, provision might be made for a tax reduction, if the rate of return over the past five years is below the agreed minimum.) The rate of the additional tax should be graduated so that as earnings rise above the minimum agreed level, the host government would receive an increasing share of the higher earnings. Provision might also be made for the review of other aspects of the agreement, but renegotiation should be limited to those clauses specifically subject to renegotiation. In return for a periodic review provision, the government should pledge not to request a renegotiation of contract conditions between the review periods nor to demand retroactive changes in the agreement. Alternatively, the periodic reviews might be left open-ended, with no guidelines or limitations on the nature of the renegotiations other than stipulating that renegotiation would take place only during designated periods, say, every five or six years. While less satisfactory to the company, such an arrangement would at least avoid the continuous conflict and uncertainty which has so often impaired production or led companies to follow practices inconsistent with the long-run maximization of revenues.[21]

---

[21] For example, companies threatened with drastic changes in contract provisions may delay necessary investments or they may be led to engage in mining practices designed to maximize current revenues but which reduce the useful life of the mine. The latter may occur when companies concentrate on mining the highest-grade ores in a manner which prevents lower-grade ores from being mined economically later on.

HOST COUNTRY BENEFITS FROM
FOREIGN MINING INVESTMENT

The governments of host countries have been increasingly insistent on maximizing the contribution of mining enterprises to the economic and social welfare of their countries. Their strategy is to pay no more than the going international price for the inputs provided by the foreign investor in developing and producing the country's mineral resources, which are regarded as belonging to the host country. In applying this strategy they often undervalue the inputs of the foreign investor or seek to acquire these inputs separately in the form of capital, management, and technology rather than as a foreign investment package. As a rule, however, the value of the package is substantially greater than the international market value of its components.

In most developing countries foreign investment in mining is regarded as a contract between the government and the foreign investor for the development and production of the resources, the contract running for a limited number of years under conditions established by the government as contractor. The conditions include not only the division of the net earnings negotiated with a view to providing the investor no more than is necessary to attract his services, but also a broad list of obligations and constraints such as maximizing the employment (and training) of domestic employees at all levels, purchasing domestic material inputs when they are available, providing a large number of fringe benefits to domestic labor, protecting the environment, and submitting to government controls over marketing and the disposition of export proceeds.

The benefits of a foreign investment to the host country can be measured in a number of ways, and a full discussion of benefits and costs is beyond the scope of this study. However, each of the case studies includes a section on the contribution of the foreign mining enterprise in terms of *retained value*, or that portion of gross revenues accruing to the host country in the form of taxes, dividends, payments to domestic shareholders, wages, salaries, and fringe benefits, domestic purchases of goods and services, and other transfers to the domestic economy. The share of retained value in gross revenue tends to rise over time as the external indebtedness is paid off, expatriates are replaced by domestic employees, domestic purchases increase, and tax revenues rise. In the case of the Toquepala mine, retained value was only about 30 percent of gross revenue during the first six years of operations, but increased rapidly thereafter so that by 1972 retained value was over 60 percent of gross revenue. For the Bougainville mine, retained value was only 24 percent during the initial period of operations—April 1972–December 1973—but under the recently renegotiated tax arrangements retained value will be in excess of 50 percent in 1974 and will vary between 50 and 60 percent after 1978, depending upon the price of copper and the net earnings of the company. In contract negotiations and renegotiations the host governments seek to maximize retained value, but if they are wise, they will seek to maximize the absolute amount of retained value rather than their relative share of the gross revenue pie.

II

The Toquepala and Bougainville Mines: Case Histories in the Economics of Copper Mining

2
A Brief History
of the
Toquepala Project

DISCOVERY AND EXPLORATION

The Toquepala mine is located above the 10,000-ft. level in a mountainous desert region of southern Peru. It is 56 air miles from the Pacific Coast and about the same distance from the Chilean border. A few miles north of Toquepala are two other large ore bodies: Cuajone, currently being developed by the same firm that developed Toquepala, the Southern Peru Copper Corporation (SPCC); and Quellaveco, which was explored by the SPCC but was taken over by the Peruvian government in January 1971. Toquepala is one of the world's largest open-pit mines, having a current capacity of about 150,000 short tons of copper content per year. During 1972 the mine produced an average of about 170,000 tons of ore and waste per day for 278 days, with an average ore grade of 1.2 percent.

The existence of copper deposits at Toquepala has been known at least since the beginning of the nineteenth century.[1] But early geologists and mining engineers visiting the deposits did not regard it as capable of being mined economically because of its low copper content, averaging about 1.25 percent copper sulfide. During the early part of the present century, a number of people filed claims to the deposit, but the claims were allowed to expire. In 1937 a claim was filed by Juan Oviedo Villegas who subsequently optioned the property to Cerro de Pasco. Cerro de Pasco did some exploratory work but

[1] For information on the early history of Toquepala, see Norman Carignan, "Southern Peru Copper Corporation—New Wealth for Peru," *Peruvian Times, Special Toquepala Supplement* (June 28, 1957), p. xviii; and Sheldon P. Wimpfen, "How the Toquepala Project Runs," *Peruvian Times* (July 4, 1969), p. 5.

reportedly gave up the option in August 1940. In 1941 the option was taken up by the Northern Peru Mining and Smelting Company, a wholly-owned subsidiary of the American Smelting and Refining Company (ASARCO). However, Cerro de Pasco subsequently claimed 50 percent ownership of the property (as a consequence of an agreement with Señor Oviedo's partner) and initiated litigation against Northern Peru in September 1941. This case was finally decided by the Peruvian Supreme Court in favor of Northern Peru in November 1948. Exploration was interrupted in the early 1940s, pending the outcome of the litigation with Cerro de Pasco, but by 1952 some $6 million had been expended for exploration and evaluation, and an additional $6 million was expended prior to the beginning of construction of the mine in 1955. These expenditures were undertaken without a mine development agreement with the Peruvian government, but the company held a mining claim and an exploration concession under the Peruvian Mining Code plus title to the smelter site at Ilo on the Peruvian coast. Northern Peru had also acquired claims on Quellaveco, but the nearby Cuajone deposit was held by Cerro de Pasco.

NEGOTIATIONS WITH THE EXPORT–IMPORT BANK

By early 1952 the ASARCO had completed a preliminary evaluation of the Toquepala project, and in March 1952 company officials approached the Defense Materials Procurement Agency (DMPA) regarding a loan to finance the development of the mine. The cost of mine, mill, and smelter, together with transportation facilities and other infrastructure capable of producing in excess of 100,000 tons of copper metal content per year, was estimated at $166 million. The ASARCO proposed that it would provide $46 million from its own funds, including $6 million already invested, and the remaining $120 million was to be provided by a loan from the U.S. government. Officials of the DMPA were favorably disposed to the granting of a loan for the mine, since they were convinced domestic U.S. copper-producing capacity was not likely to increase appreciably over the 1952 levels, and growing U.S. consumption requirements would need to be met increasingly by imports.[2]

[2] The Paley Commission Report projected that U.S. copper mine production would decline from 907,000 short tons in 1950 to 800,000 short tons in 1975, and that by 1975 net U.S. imports would be about 1 million short tons. See The President's Materials Policy Commission, *Resources for Freedom*, vol. II (June 1952), p. 36.

On July 10, 1952, the ASARCO presented a statement to a conference of U.S. government representatives, including officials from the DMPA, the Defense Production Administration (DPA), the Departments of State and Commerce, and the Export–Import Bank. This statement summarized the project evaluation and detailed the capital expenditure estimates and the projected operating cost per pound of copper produced by Toquepala. Later in that same month the ASARCO made a formal request to the DMPA for a loan of $120 million for the development of Toquepala. During the following months both the DMPA and the Export–Import Bank made detailed investigations of the proposal and of the outlook for the future Free World supply and demand for copper, particularly for the United States. In February 1953, the DMPA transmitted to the Export–Import Bank a "certificate of essentiality" (approved by the DPA) for the Toquepala loan, on condition that a maximum of 50 percent of the entire production of the Toquepala mine be optioned for purchase by the U.S. government. Following negotiations with the ASARCO, a proposed contract was agreed upon in mid-April 1953 which provided that $60 million would be loaned under Section 302 of the Defense Production Act and another $60 million under the Export–Import Bank Act of 1945. The ASARCO would invest $40 million but would not be asked to guarantee repayment of the loans. The loans would be repaid in fifty semiannual installments beginning in July 1959 (after the construction period was completed) at an interest rate of 5 percent per annum. Subsequently, the Export–Import Bank sent the proposed loan contract for approval to the National Advisory Council on International Monetary and Financial Problems (NAC). Meanwhile, in December 1952, the ASARCO organized the Southern Peru Copper Corporation (SPCC) as a Delaware corporation. The SPCC subsequently entered into the mining agreement with the Peruvian government for the development of the Toquepala mine and negotiated the credit agreement with the Export–Import Bank. Initially, the SPCC was a wholly-owned subsidiary of the ASARCO; the partnership arrangement which was to include three other mining companies along with the mining claims to Cuajone (originally held by Cerro de Pasco) was not formed until September 1955.

Following the submission of the proposed loan contract to the NAC for approval, the ASARCO undertook further engineering work and cost estimation, the final estimate for the original project being completed in December 1953. The new capital requirements, including working capital, were estimated to be $177.4 million as compared with the original estimate of $160 million. These capital expenditures, coupled with an Export–Import Bank requirement that interest accruing during the construction period be compounded, resulted in a capital requirement so large that the project was not regarded as financially attractive. Preliminary estimates were then made for a mine with a lower initial rate of production in the hope that profits could be used to expand the operation later on. However, the outcome proved to be unattractive, since fixed charges for amortization and interest on the lesser amount of capital were regarded as too large in relation to projected current income. An analysis was then made of the feasibility of constructing a mine with an initial mining rate of 30,000 tons of ore per day, resulting in an annual production of 139,000 tons of refined copper for the first ten years and 100,000 tons thereafter. (This was in contrast to the original program of 21,600 tons per day and an initial refined copper output of 100,000 tons per year.) A preliminary estimate of the cost of this project called for a new capital investment of $196 million. With this new project, output could be increased by 35 percent, with a 12 percent increase in capital outlays. Such a mine was regarded as economically feasible. (Later the estimate of copper output was reduced to 120,000 tons per year for the first ten years, followed by an annual output of 90,000 tons in the second ten-year period.)

Meanwhile, since the $60 million loan which was to be provided under the Defense Production Act was no longer available, the U.S. government financing would need to come entirely from the Export–Import Bank. Therefore, in August 1954, the ASARCO outlined to the Export–Import Bank a financial plan for Toquepala for the raising of $196 million in new capital, half of which would be contributed by the ASARCO and one or more partners and the other half by the Export–Import Bank. This proposal was discussed by the ASARCO officials with the secretary of the treasury on September 7, 1954. After further discussions with Export–Import Bank officials, the bank advised the ASARCO on November 5, 1954, that it had approved in principle the extension of a credit not to exceed $100 million plus capitalized interest to assist in the development of the Toquepala project. An important condition of the credit was that not less than $95 million, inclusive of the sums expended to date, would be invested in the project by the ASARCO or by the ASARCO and its partner firms. Another condition was that the project would be completed without additional financing by the bank and all investment previously made or hereafter required in addition to the loan from the bank would be subordinated to the bank's loan. Advances under the proposed credit would be repayable in semiannual installments over a period of not more than fifteen years following the initial five-year construction period and would bear a rate of interest of not less than 6 percent per annum, such interest to be compounded during the five-year construction period and added to the principal of the loan. On April 25, 1955, the ASARCO informed the Export–Import Bank that preliminary arrangements had been made for the investment of not less than $95 million by the ASARCO and its partners, the Cerro Corporation, the Newmont Mining Corporation and the Phelps Dodge Corporation. Meanwhile, a mine development agreement had been signed between the government of Peru and the SPCC. However, the final credit agreement between the Export–Import Bank and the SPCC was delayed until September 30, 1955.

The history of the negotiations on the Export–Import Bank loan for Toquepala was closely associated with the foreign economic policy of the United States. The U.S. government's initial enthusiasm for the project in 1952 stemmed largely from its concern for an adequate supply of copper, but the project was also regarded as a means of promoting Latin American economic development. However, at the beginning of the Eisenhower Administration, U.S. policy changed, and DPA loans became available only for projects required for stockpile purposes. Moreover, the concern for U.S. copper supplies declined with the termination of the Korean War and with a more favorable outlook for domestic supplies of copper. Also, in 1953, the secretary of the treasury announced a policy of reducing the loan activities of the Export–Import Bank so the argument advanced in 1952, that a loan for the Toquepala mine would promote U.S. interests in Latin American development, no longer carried weight within the U.S. government.[3] However, beginning with Secretary of State Dulles's address of March 4, 1954, at the Conference of the Organization of American States in Caracas, Venezuela, and followed later by a statement by Secretary of the Treasury Humphrey in Rio de Janeiro, the 1953 policy was changed, and the Export–Import Bank began making long-term loans for Latin American development, including loans in support of U.S. direct foreign investment. The decision announced by the Export–Import Bank on November 5, 1954, approving in principle the $100 million loan for Toquepala, was not unrelated to the change in U.S. foreign economic policy. However, the Export–Import Bank's decision

[3] According to the policy adopted by the NAC in August 1953, the Export–Import Bank was to confine its activities largely to short-term loans for assisting exporters, leaving the long-term lending field to the World Bank. For a discussion of this policy, see testimony of Samuel C. Waugh, president of the Export–Import Bank in *Extension of Export–Import Bank Act*, Hearings before the Senate Subcommittee of the Committee on Banking and Currency, 84 Cong., 2 sess. (June 8, 1956), pp. 21–22.

provided for a 6 percent loan, whereas the negotiations in 1952 referred to an interest rate of 4.5 percent.

In a memorandum presented to the Export–Import Bank, dated February 1, 1955, the ASARCO argued that a 6 percent rate of interest was not consistent with the government's announced policy of encouraging U.S. direct private investment in Latin America. The company also showed that other Export–Import Bank loans, as well as those from the World Bank, had been made for similar purposes at substantially lower rates in 1954. However, this memorandum did not go so far as to state that the ASARCO would be unable to go ahead with the project with a 6 percent loan from the Export–Import Bank or that Toquepala would lose money if it paid that rate. Evidently the company's argument had an impact since the loan was finally made at an interest rate of $5\frac{1}{8}$ percent.

NEGOTIATION OF THE CONCESSION AGREEMENT

In January 1949, shortly after exploration work began on a significant scale at Toquepala, R. W. Straus, chairman of the ASARCO, and R. F. Goodwin, the vice president, met with General Odría, president of Peru, who gave assurances that if the company decided to develop either Toquepala or Quellaveco, the government of Peru would do everything in its power to aid the enterprise. Similar assurances were given in May 1950 by members of the Peruvian cabinet, including the ministers of finance, development, and aviation. Prior to the initiation of negotiations with the DMPA and the Export–Import Bank, officials of the ASARCO had preliminary discussions with Peruvian officials regarding a bilateral agreement with the government covering the rights and obligations of the company for the construction and operation of mines on the copper porphyry properties of Toquepala and Quellaveco. In a memorandum to the DMPA, dated July 18, 1952, the ASARCO stated that the government was enthusiastic about the project and that there were no major issues outstanding between it and the company. The memorandum further stated that the company was prepared to operate under the tax rate and other regulations of the existing Peruvian mining code (Mining Code of 1950), and that no special concessions or exemptions were sought other than those consistent with the provisions of the Mining Code relating to "marginal mining operations" (Article 56). However, the memorandum did state that certain points required clarification and prior agreement with the government. These had to do with import duties and consular fees on equipment imported in connection with the project; arrangements regarding the management and public use of the port and railroad; and the free availability of the foreign exchange from exports of copper for meeting the company's obligations. All of these were successfully negotiated, and the results were incorporated in the bilateral agreement between the government of Peru and the SPCC, signed on November 11, 1954.

The tax arrangements under the bilateral agreement were in accordance with the Mining Code of 1950. The tax rate, including the tax on the company's net profits plus the tax on the transfer of dividends abroad, was limited to 30 percent of net earnings (after deducting amortization, depreciation, and depletion) until the capital investment was fully amortized out of net profits. Also, actual tax payments were partly deferred during the amortization period, being limited to 10 percent of net profits during the preceding year. However, the SPCC was subject to a 4 percent export tax on the net value of sales each year, and this amount was to be deducted from the income tax due for that year. At the time of the agreement, the normal corporate tax was graduated according to the amount of net profits up to 20 percent, plus a graduated tax on excess profits (in excess of 10 percent of net investment) up to 20 percent of excess profits over 1 million soles. In addition, there was a 30 percent tax on dividend transfers. Depending upon the calculation of excess profits, the normal tax would have constituted an effective tax rate of up to 54.5 percent, including the dividend transfer tax, as contrasted with the maximum rate of 30 percent guaranteed to the SPCC during the amortization period.

According to the formula provided in the agreement, the SPCC would not have been subject to a tax in excess of 30 percent, at least until 1969. However, pressure was brought on the company to agree to taxation at the normal rate beginning in 1968, during which year the effective tax rate (including the tax on transferred dividends) was 54.5 percent. In 1970 this rate was raised to 68 percent.

At the time of the agreement, Peruvian mining legislation provided for a depletion allowance equal to 15 percent of the export value of metal. The allowance was limited to 50 percent of net profit subject to tax before depletion. In addition, depreciation on plant and equipment and amortization of capitalized exploration and mine development expenditures were deductible from taxable income. Buildings and equipment are depreciated by the SPCC over an estimated depreciable life of five to thirty-three years, except for automotive equipment, which is depreciated over three years. Mine development is charged to earnings at a rate per ton estimated to amortize the development costs over a period of approximately ten years from the beginning of operations. Under the Mining Code of 1950, depletion was not required to be reinvested in the mine, but this was later changed so that depletion not reinvested within three years is subject to normal income and dividend transfer taxes. However, according to the agreement, this would not apply to Toquepala until the initial investment in the mine was fully amortized out of net earnings. In 1967 the SPCC, under pressure from the Peruvian government, agreed to include in its 1967 taxable income all depletion deducted in its tax returns for the years 1963, 1965, and 1966 which had not been reinvested in exploration or development. Under a special agreement for the development of Cuajone reached in 1969, the SPCC was permitted to invest its 15 percent depletion allowance from Toquepala without tax in the Cuajone project.

One of the important provisions in the 1954 agreement was that all equipment and materials for the construction and operation of Toquepala and Quellaveco would be free from import duties except for a 7.5 percent ad valorem consular fee. However, during the construction period, payment of the 7.5 percent construction fee was to be deferred until profits had been applied to the complete amortization of capital expenditures. Nevertheless, in 1968, the company agreed to pay these consular fees, totaling over $6 million, earlier than had been provided for in the agreement.

Another important financial issue in the agreement had to do with restrictions on the use of foreign exchange from exports. The Export–Import Bank was naturally concerned that there be no constraint on the use of the SPCC's revenues for servicing the Export–Import Bank loan. According to the agreement, the Peruvian government stipulated during the period of amortization of the loans from the Export–Import Bank, the amortization of the advances by the ASARCO and its partners, as well as the amortization of the company's own capital, that

> [The] company may dispose without restriction of any kind, of the foreign exchange resulting from its exports which it will require to attend to the following payments: (a) for servicing the amortization and interest on said credit operations; (b) for the payment of fees for guaranteeing the loans; (c) for amortization of its own capital; and (d) for all other requirements as provided for in Law 10905. . . . In cases which are referred to involving amortization, payments of interest and payments of guarantee fees on the loans, the sole obligation of the company will be to submit documentary proof of these obligations which have to be met.

Commencing in October 1967, while service payments on the Export–Import Bank loan were still being made, the Peruvian government reestablished foreign exchange controls which restrict the convertibility of Peruvian soles into foreign currencies. U.S. dollars received for sales made by the SPCC and other companies exporting from Peru must be deposited with the Central Reserve Bank of Peru and can be used subsequently, when authorized by the government, for payment of foreign currency obligations and remittance of profits. In October 1971, the government's commercial entity for the mining industry, Empresa Minera del Peru, became the sole marketer of Peruvian mineral products.

CAPITAL REQUIREMENTS AND THE MOBILIZATION OF FUNDS

According to the ASARCO's original proposal based on a total capital cost of $166 million, the company would invest $46 million in Toquepala and the remainder would be financed by a U.S. government loan. As has been noted, subsequent engineering analysis showed that an economically feasible mine would require new capital expenditures of $196 million, in addition to the nearly $10 million that had already been spent by the ASARCO through 1954. Moreover, with the withdrawal of the $60 million prospective loan to be provided under the Defense Production Act, the Export–Import Bank indicated that it would provide no more than half of the total new funds required for the project. Since the ASARCO had determined that it would not provide more than $40 million in new capital outlays, it became necessary to find other equity partners. By bringing Cerro Corporation and Newmont Mining into the project, it was possible to add their claims to the nearby Cuajone ore body to those of the SPCC.[4] When these claims were combined with Toquepala and Quellaveco, they totaled more than a billion tons of ore, averaging over 1 percent of copper. Eventually, all three ore bodies would be exploited, beginning with Toquepala.

Under an agreement of September 30, 1955, among the SPCC and the four parent companies, the ASARCO transferred to the SPCC the Toquepala and Quellaveco properties (held by the former's subsidiary, Northern Peru), and Cerro and Newmont transferred their interests in

---

[4] Bringing Phelps Dodge into the project made it possible to utilize that company's expertise in developing and mining large open-pit ore bodies.

Cuajone. The capitalized value of these properties was $12 million, based on the amount spent on the properties prior to the agreement with the SPCC. In addition, the partners provided $20.2 million in new equity capital. The agreement also provided that the partners would contribute up to $65.8 million in advances to the SPCC, these advances being subordinate to the Export–Import Bank loan. These advances, plus the $20.2 million in new equity, totaled $86 million, which, with anticipated suppliers' credits, represented about half of the additional capital then believed to be required for the construction of Toquepala, with the other half to be supplied by the $100 million Export–Import Bank loan.

The actual construction of the mine cost somewhat more than was anticipated at the time of the September 30, 1955, agreement, so that advances by the partners totaled $74.8 million instead of the $65.8 million originally planned, and there was a small increase in the provision of new equity. The Export–Import Bank loans totaled $109.8 million plus $9.8 million in credits representing interest accrued prior to the making of debt service payments, for a total Export–Import Bank contribution of $119.6 million. Finally, there were suppliers' loans amounting to $10.1 million. Thus the total capital investment in the SPCC to the end of 1959 was financed as follows:

Source of investment	Millions U.S. dollars
Equity	32.6
Suppliers' credits	10.1
Advances by partners	74.8
Export-Import Bank loans	119.6
Total	U.S.$237.1

The final distribution of the equity shares was as follows:

Company	No. of shares	Percentage of total shares outstanding
ASARCO	167,890	51.50
Cerro	72,535	22.25
Newmont Mining	33,415	10.25
Phelps Dodge	52,160	16.00
Total	326,000	100.00

THE PRODUCTION PERIOD

Toquepala came into production in 1960, producing 52 million short tons of materials, including 9.5 million short tons of ore from which

Table 4. Production, Cost, and Price Data for Toquepala, 1960–73

Year	Blister copper production (short tons)	Production cost per pound[a] (U.S. cents)	Total cost per pound[b] (U.S. cents)	Average price per pound[c] (U.S. cents)
1960	145,115	9.0	n.a.	28.7
1961	160,012	9.1	n.a.	28.4
1962	126,236	10.4	19.3	29.0
1963	131,664	11.0	18.6	29.0
1964	127,489	12.1	19.5	31.3
1965	121,289	12.6	20.4	36.3
1966	125,641	14.2	20.2	53.9
1967	139,450	14.1	21.0	48.1
1968	147,721	13.5	19.6	49.4
1969	134,234	15.1	22.6	66.9
1970	142,894	15.6	22.0	55.8
1971	135,627	16.6	24.3	47.7
1972	138,187	18.2	25.3	45.8
1973	128,488	21.8	29.5	87.3

[a] Excludes amortization, depletion, depreciation, and interest on loans.

[b] The total cost per pound of refined copper includes direct and indirect costs, refining and delivery, depletion, depreciation, mine amortization and interest but less credits for silver and molybdenum and miscellaneous income.

[c] Average price of copper obtained on sales.

145,115 short tons of blister copper were obtained, plus smaller amounts of silver and molybdenum. Total production cost per pound of copper was approximately 9 cents in 1960 and 1961, somewhat less than the 1954 estimate of 11 cents per pound for the first ten years of production. In 1961 blister copper output was 160,012 short tons, the highest that has ever been attained. In 1962 output declined to 126,239, rising to 131,664 tons in 1963, and thereafter fluctuating between 125,641 tons (in 1966) and 147,721 tons (in 1968); in 1972 output was 138,187 tons (Table 4). Variation in output reflects mainly time lost from strikes (forty-three days in 1972) and the grade of ore mined. In order to maintain output in the face of a decline in ore grade, a 35 percent expansion of the Toquepala mill was completed in 1965. Strikes at the Toquepala mine and at the smelter at Ilo have had a serious impact on output in some years. In 1969, fifty days' production was lost at the mine with a consequent shutdown of thirty-one days at the smelter due to the lack of concentrates. In 1971–72, strikes caused a loss of thirty-seven and thirty days, respectively, at the mine and forty-one and forty-three days, respectively, at the smelter (see Table 5).

Production costs have risen steadily throughout the 1960–72 period, rising to 18.2 cents per pound of copper in 1972 and an estimated 21.8

Table 5. Days Lost from Strikes at the Toquepala Mine and at the Smelter in Ilo, 1966–73

Year	Toquepala mine	Smelter
1973	52	46
1972	30	43
1971	37	41
1970	21	0
1969	50	0[a]
1968	6	0
1967	0	0
1966	26	32

[a] However, there was a smelter stoppage for thirty-one days due to lack of concentrates.

cents for 1973.[5] Over the 1960–72 period labor costs rose by more than 4 cents per pound. In 1973 the total cost of recoverable copper, including direct and indirect costs, refining and delivery, amortization, depreciation, and depletion, but minus credits for silver and molybdenum and miscellaneous income, was 29.5 cents per pound, having risen from 18.6 cents per pound in 1963. (These figures exclude income taxes.)

Fortunately for the SPCC, copper prices rose by substantially more than production costs and averaged 2.5 times the 18.5 cents per pound initially projected as the average price of copper during the first ten years of production.[6] A rough calculation of actual production costs in 1972 yields an amount slightly less than total sales revenue at 18.5 cents-per-pound copper, leaving nothing for interest, depreciation, depletion, income taxes, and net profits. Moreover, it would not have been possible to maintain Toquepala's output in the absence of the more than $45 million in capital additions during the 1960–72 period. Because of the rise in copper prices, Toquepala has proved to be profitable both to the government, which received $262 million in income taxes plus $27 million in other taxes, and to the stockholders, who received $278 million in dividends, over the 1960–72 period. In addition, all but $3.6 million of the Export–Import Bank loan had been paid off with interest by the end of 1972, together with the $74.8 million in stockholders' advances and the $10 million of suppliers' credits. Also, $83 million had been invested in Cuajone by the end

---

[5] Production costs include indirect costs which are administration and service facilities for workers (schools, hospitals, housing, etc.), but exclude depletion, depreciation, mine amortization, interest on loans, and income taxes.

[6] The basis for the 18.5 cents-per-pound price for copper, projected in 1952, will be discussed in Chapter 3.

of 1972, and $45 million in capital additions had been added to Toquepala.

Marketing of Products

Prior to 1971, 60–75 percent of Toquepala's output was sold to the shareholders in accordance with contractual arrangements, and the rest was marketed by the Southern Peru Copper Sales Corporation. However, effective October 14, 1971, the government declared that Empresa Minera del Peru (Minero Peru) would become the sole marketer of Peruvian mineral products. In February 1972 an agreement was reached with Minero Peru, whereby up to 20 percent of Toquepala's blister copper production would be marketed by that organization and the balance by the company with a commission paid Minero Peru. Thus, during 1972, SPCC shareholders purchased 60.9 percent of the output, Southern Peru Copper Sales Corporation marketed 21.5 percent, and the remaining 17.6 percent was marketed by Minero Peru. As a consequence of the new arrangement marketing costs have been increased, since the state enterprise receives a commission on all sales whether or not it handles them directly. To date, all the SPCC copper marketed by Minero Peru has been purchased from the SPCC on commercial terms. The bilateral agreement of December 1969 between the government of Peru and the SPCC for the construction of Cuajone provided that mine production from Cuajone was to be marketed by the company without restriction during the period of investment recovery. However, the long-term sales contracts for Cuajone's output were negotiated and executed with the full participation of Minero Peru.

The Cuajone Bilateral Agreement

The Cuajone bilateral agreement of December 1969 between the Peruvian government and the SPCC presents some interesting contrasts with the Toquepala agreement of 1954. First, the mine construction and installation program together with cost estimates for each expenditure category are set forth in considerable detail in the Cuajone agreement as contrasted with the far less comprehensive treatment of the investment plan (without itemized cost estimates) in the Toquepala agreement. Under the Toquepala agreement the company was required to initiate construction within eighteen months of its signing. However, for the Cuajone mine the company was obligated to submit to the government a scheme for financing the investment plan set forth in the agreement, together with copies of the financing agreements. (Arrangements for the full financing of Cuajone were not completed until January 1975 by which time nearly $200 million had been invested in Cuajone, financed by cash flow from Toquepala.)

The Toquepala agreement allows the company to dispose of foreign exchange earnings without restriction for the servicing of foreign loans, the amortization of its own capital, and for certain other purposes during the period of investment recovery. The Cuajone agreement, on the other hand, provides a compromise between full surrender of foreign exchange proceeds by the company and complete government control. Although the procedure is rather complicated, in brief, it provides for the depositing of foreign exchange proceeds from minerals in an account with a New York bank. While this account is in the name of the Central Reserve Bank of Peru, the company irrevocably is authorized to draw monthly amounts equivalent to profits, depreciation, amortization and other sums stipulated in the agreement. The text of the irrevocable order to the New York bank is provided in the agreement.

In the Toquepala agreement the maximum tax rate (corporate income plus profits transfer tax) that could be charged during the amortization period was 30 percent, while under the Cuajone agreement this maximum is 47.5 percent. However, in the Toquepala agreement amortization of invested capital referred to amortization out of after-tax earnings (after deducting depreciation, amortization, depletion, and all taxes). In the Cuajone agreement the period of investment recovery is much shorter since investment is recovered out of capital consumption allowances, that is, depreciation and amortization. The Cuajone agreement also provides that for the first six years following investment recovery the maximum tax is 54.5 percent of taxable income.

The Toquepala agreement exempted the importation of all equipment and materials required for the construction, preparation and exploitation of Toquepala from all import duties and additional charges with the exception of the consular fee amounting to 7.5 percent ad valorem. In addition, there was a provision for the deferral of the 7.5 percent ad valorem consular fee until after the capital had been amortized. Under the Cuajone agreement exemption from import duties apparently applies only during the construction period, and there is no exemption for the 8 percent ad valorem consular fee.

In general, the Cuajone agreement is much more specific with respect to the obligations of the company in such matters as the training and hiring of local labor and the purchase of goods and services of national origin. Thus, in the Toquepala agreement, the company was exempted from certain labor and local purchase requirements, while in the Cuajone agreement the company assumes specific obligations with respect to both employment and local purchases. For example, the company is to acquire materials of national origin provided they are of comparable quality and the prices are competitive with imports. As the agreement states, "The price shall be considered competitive when the value of the national product does not exceed by more than 25 percent the CIF value of the similar foreign product."

CUAJONE AND QUELLAVECO

Cuajone

In December 1969 the SPCC signed a contract with the Peruvian government providing for the development of the Cuajone ore body and the construction of facilities then estimated to cost $355 million. Cuajone is an open-pit mine designed to produce 170,000 short tons of blister copper per year. Under the contract the company was obligated to spend or commit $25 million for the project by October 1, 1971, and to complete the project within six and a half years. By the end of 1971 total expenditures on Cuajone amounted to approximately $46 million, and another $37 million was expended on Cuajone during 1972, bringing the total at the end of 1972 to nearly $83 million, including the cost of mineral lands. The work plan for Cuajone filed with the Peruvian government called for the expenditures or commitment of $60 million during the calendar year 1973. In order to maintain the agreed level of capital expenditures for Cuajone pending the raising of the large amount of external capital required, the SPCC decided to employ all of its cash flow from Toquepala for investment in Cuajone beginning July 1972, and by late 1974 the SPCC had committed $190 million of its own funds to Cuajone, plus additional amounts in short-term credits for a total of $341 million. By this time the total cost of the project, including the expansion of the SPCC's smelter at Ilo, was estimated to be $620 million, or 75 percent above the 1969 estimate.

Meanwhile the SPCC conducted negotiations with commercial banks, equipment suppliers, and the Export–Import Bank for over $400 million in loans and credits to complete the construction of Cuajone. In addition, the SPCC negotiated long-term contracts for the sale of about 100,000 tons of copper annually to buyers other than stockholders. In early January 1975—five years after the development contract for

Cuajone was signed—it was announced that all of these interrelated negotiations had been completed and that Cuajone was expected to begin commercial production in 1976. It was also announced that a Dutch firm, Billiton B.V., would make an equity investment of $25 million, or 11.5 percent of the total equity in Cuajone, with the remaining 88.5 percent ($191 million) being held by the SPCC.[7] The $404 million in debt capital will come from the following sources: $200 million from a consortium of twenty-nine banks, led by the Chase Manhattan Bank; $140 million in long-term credits, including $75 million in loans and guarantees from the Export–Import Bank; $54 million arranged by copper purchasers, who have contracted for a substantial portion of Cuajone's output; and $10 million from the International Finance Corporation (IFC). The inclusion of the IFC in the financing undoubtedly helped to persuade some of the other creditors.

Cuajone will not only be one of the world's largest copper mines, but will be the most expensive in terms of initial capital cost. Yet a capital cost of about $3,650 per annual ton of copper metal is not high by modern standards, and given its ore grade of over 1 percent (with reserves estimated at 468 million tons of sulfide ore), it should prove to be a profitable mine for many years. When in full operation, Cuajone will employ an estimated 1,800 workers.

It is rather remarkable that a Peruvian mine the size of Cuajone will be nearly 100 percent foreign owned.[8] Given Peru's recent history of expropriation—in December 1973 the Peruvian government expropriated Cerro de Pasco, one of Peru's oldest and largest foreign-owned metal mining firms, and had previously expropriated several other large foreign investments—the apparent risk to the foreign investors in Cuajone is too obvious for comment. On the other hand, the Peruvian government is very anxious for Cuajone to be built, and it is unlikely that the amount of capital required could have been mobilized and the mine constructed within the projected time period by a Peruvian government enterprise. Another factor working in favor of the foreign owners of Cuajone is that the Peruvian government is hoping to attract more than a billion dollars in external capital to develop several large mining properties held by the government's mining enterprise, Minero Peru, in an effort to triple Peru's output of copper over the next few years.

[7] "Southern Peru Gets Financing for Copper Mine," *Wall Street Journal,* January 6, 1975, p. 6. Some of the other facts in the above discussion were derived from an article entitled "Cuajone's Financing Near Completion," *Andean Times,* July 19, 1974, p. 6.

[8] At the end of 1974 the Mining Community (discussed on pages 55–56) owned 9 percent of the SPCC's shares and will eventually own 50 percent.

Quellaveco

The November 1954 agreement between the SPCC and the Peruvian government provided for the construction of Quellaveco as the second phase of the program but did not put a specific time limit on the beginning of construction, as was the case for Toquepala (eighteen months from the time of the agreement). However, in 1969 the Peruvian government required all holders of unworked mining concessions to submit plans for beginning production by 1975 or to forfeit their concessions. And on August 14, 1970, the Peruvian government ordered the companies to present "critical path method-planned projects" for their concessions by September 1970, and, if the plans were accepted, the companies would be given until December 31, 1970, to arrange financing for their projects and to present proof of the availability of funds for financing. This proved to be an impossible timetable for the SPCC, especially in finding the financing for the construction of Cuajone, which required a total outlay of over $500 million. On January 4, 1971, the Peruvian government declared that the SPCC had not complied with the law requiring submission of documentation assuring the financing of the Quellaveco project, and, therefore, this mining concession reverted to the government. However, in its planning the SPCC regarded Quellaveco as an additional ore reserve to be mined for processing at the Toquepala or Cuajone mills.

THE SYSTEM OF MINING COMMUNITIES

A major innovation in the General Mining Law of June 1971 was the provision for a system of Mining Communities (Comunidades Mineras), under which mining companies must set aside 10 percent of their pretax profits annually, 4 percent of which is paid in cash to the communities and 6 percent in shares of the company. However, only 20 percent of each of these amounts will be retained by the individual community; the remaining 30 percent will go to the nationwide Comunidade de Compensación Minera, which will distribute the cash and shares to all of the individual Mining Communities in Peru. Each mine worker receives a cash payment annually based on the number of days worked, and when a Comunidade has acquired 50 percent ownership of the capital of the company, the individual workers are to receive shares in the company. Ostensibly the purpose of this arrangement is to provide for worker ownership of the mining company. However, a more important purpose may be to provide a means by which Peruvian residents will eventually own 50 percent of the shares of the mining companies. According to the regulations issued in April 1972, the SPCC was required to provide certificates of participation in a newly organized Peruvian branch of the SPCC amounting to $3 million plus an additional $2 million to be paid in cash (Peruvian soles) for 1972. For 1971 the total contribution to the Mining Communities was $2.8 million, of which $1.8 million took the form of participation certificates with the balance in cash.

3
Economic and Political Factors in the Investment Decision for the Toquepala Project

In this chapter I shall apply the criteria, discussed in Part I, relating to investment decisions by foreign mining companies to the investment in Toquepala. By most standards the investment climate in Peru during the critical decision-making period, 1952–55, was excellent. Although, like most Latin American countries, Peru had a history of political instability, political control was rather firmly in the hands of the military and Peru's "forty wealthy families." Except for the long-standing constitutional issue over the International Petroleum Company (IPC) owned by the Standard Oil Company of New Jersey,[1] foreign investors were not threatened, even by the leading left-of-center party, APRA. There was considerable economic instability in the late 1940s accompanied by inflation and exchange controls, but beginning in 1949 the administration of Gen. Manuel Odría, president of Peru, put into effect a series of measures that gave confidence to foreign investors. These included (1) the adoption of a free exchange system with unrestricted transfer of profits and repatriation of capital; (2) the dismantling of the import licensing system; and (3) the enactment of the new mining code, establishing favorable conditions without distinction of nationality for the filing and exploitation of mining concessions. Not only did the Mining Code of 1950 provide for reduced taxes and tax deferral during the period required for the investor to recover his investment, but it also provided for a 15 percent

[1] For a fascinating story of the IPC case, see Richard N. Goodwin, "Letter from Peru," *The New Yorker Magazine* (May 17, 1969), pp. 41–109. The story begins in the early part of the nineteenth century, long before IPC was organized.

depletion allowance, something not usually found in the tax regulations of developing countries.

In the early 1950s, when the American Smelting and Refining Company (ASARCO) was considering its investment in Toquepala, several foreign companies—including Cerro de Pasco and the ASARCO subsidiary, the Northern Peru Mining Company—had been operating successfully in Peru for several decades. The Toquepala mine, even as originally conceived, represented a huge investment, one of the largest in the world outside the United States. In order to be profitable, open-pit mines producing low-grade ore must operate on a very large scale, and an enormous investment must be made over a period of five years or more before there are any revenues. Such mines cannot start on a small scale and grow, as in the case of underground mines producing relatively rich ore. Moreover, since the Toquepala mine was in a remote mountainous region, a large amount of infrastructure, including a highway, a railroad, a port, and mining communities, had to be created. The ASARCO determined, therefore, that no more than $40 million of its own capital should be invested in Toquepala plus the several million already put into the exploration of the mine. Hence, it envisaged a financial structure with a fairly high debt–equity ratio of the order of 3:1 involving new equity capital of $40 million and debt capital of $120 million. Moreover, for the mine to be viable in terms of the large indebtedness, the ASARCO believed it would need a loan with a maturity of twenty-five years or more at relatively low rates of interest. The only likely source of capital on these terms was the U.S. government, and such financing would be forthcoming only if the government were convinced that it was in the national interest of the United States to provide public assistance for the development of the mine and that the mine would not be constructed by American enterprise without government financing.

A search of the ASARCO's materials relating to the financial evaluation of the Toquepala mine in 1952 revealed estimates of capital expenditures for constructing mines of varying scale, estimates of operating costs per pound of copper disaggregated by labor and other inputs, a comparison of these cost estimates with costs elsewhere in the world, and the projection of a range of copper prices.[2] There apparently were no sophisticated internal rate-of-return projections based on cash flow analysis. The long-term price and demand projec-

___

[2] Nearly all of the financial analysis and evaluation of the proposed Toquepala mine made available to me by the ASARCO officials had been prepared for presentation to the Export–Import Bank and the Defense Materials Procurement Agency (DMPA) during the loan negotiations.

tions appear to be exceedingly cautious in terms of what actually occurred. This must be understood in the light of the economic conditions prevailing at the time when the Korean War with its heavy demand for copper was drawing to a close, and perhaps also in the light of the widespread view that the world might again experience a 1930-type depression.

PROJECTING FUTURE COPPER PRICES

In the documents supplied by the ASARCO in support of its application to the Export–Import Bank and to the DMPA for a $120 million loan for Toquepala in 1952 and early 1953, a case was made that 18.5 cents (in 1952 prices) was a conservative average (not a minimum) price per pound of copper over the next thirty years. The average U.S. domestic producers' price in 1952 was 24.2 cents, and the average price on the London Metal Exchange (LME) was 32.6 cents per pound. However, these prices were believed to reflect the heavy demand for copper during the Korean War. In 1949 the U.S. domestic producers' price was 19.2 cents per pound, and the LME price was 16.3 cents per pound. During World War II the U.S. domestic producers' price was fixed at 11.8 cents per pound, and both the U.S. producers' price and the LME price were about 10 cents per pound in 1938 (see Table 6). Justification for the pessimistic outlook for copper prices was based partly on the relationship between projected Free World copper-producing capacity for 1960 and the projected Free World demand. U.S. copper consumption was projected to rise from 1,350,000 tons in 1951 to 1,720,000 tons in 1960, and foreign consumption from 1,390,000 tons in 1959 to 1,750,000 tons in 1960, giving a total Free World consumption for 1960 of 3,470,000 tons.[3] Taking into account both the likelihood of U.S. recessions and reductions in production caused by strikes and other factors (some of which could be met from the U.S. stockpile), ASARCO officials projected a price range of 17–24 cents per pound for the years around 1960. Moreover, it was pointed out that if the U.S. government reimposed the 2 cents-per-pound duty on copper (which had been removed during the Korean War), the projected net

[3] Domestic consumption was projected partly on the basis of historic trends adjusted for the substitution of aluminum and other materials for copper, and partly on the projected increase in the Federal Reserve Board production index. The projection of Free World consumption was taken from the Paley Commission report [The President's Materials Policy Commission, *Resources for Freedom*, vol. II (June 1952), pp. 36–37].

Table 6. Annual Average of U.S. Domestic Producers' and London Metal Exchange Copper Prices, 1938–73
(U.S. cents per pound)

Year	U.S. domestic producers	LME	Year	U.S. domestic producers	LME
1938	10.0	9.9	1956	41.8	41.0
1939	11.0	10.1	1957	29.6	27.4
1940	11.3	11.2	1958	25.8	24.8
1941	11.8	11.2	1959	31.2	29.8
1942	11.8	11.2	1960	32.1	30.8
1943	11.8	11.2	1961	29.9	28.8
1944	11.8	11.2	1962	30.6	29.3
1945	11.8	11.2	1963	30.6	29.3
1946	13.8	13.9	1964	32.0	44.0
1947	21.0	16.3	1965	35.0	58.8
1948	22.0	16.8	1966	36.2	69.1
1949	19.2	16.3	1967	38.2	50.9
1950	21.3	22.4	1968	41.9	55.8
1951	24.2	27.6	1969	47.5	66.6
1952	24.2	32.6	1970	57.7	63.8
1953	28.8	30.1	1971	51.4	49.3
1954	29.7	31.2	1972	50.6	48.6
1955	37.5	43.8	1973	65.7	80.9

Sources: Metal Bulletin, Metals Week, and *Engineering and Mining Journal,* various issues.

price range for Toquepala copper would be 15–22 cents per pound. It was, therefore, believed that 18.5 cents per pound for 1960 was a reasonable average.

Looking beyond 1960, ASARCO officials referred to the Paley Commission report which speculated on the price of copper over the next twenty-five years to 1975. According to this report, "If sufficient expansion of production is achieved, the cost of copper in 1950 dollars should stay in the neighborhood of the 1950 range in the United States (18½–24½ cents)...."[4] The Paley Commission also envisaged the possibility that the price of copper might be pushed appreciably higher than the 1951–52 level of about 24 cents.

The ASARCO's supporting memoranda also projected U.S. and foreign copper production in 1957 at various prices per pound. For example, at 18 cents per pound world copper production for 1957 was estimated at about 3.1 million tons, while at 24 cents per pound production would rise to nearly 3.4 million tons.[5] Relating these estimates

[4] Ibid., pp. 37–38.
[5] Actually the ASARCO's projections of both Free World consumption and capacity for 1960 proved to be far wide of the mark. Estimated Free World copper-producing capacity was 4.3 million short tons in 1960, and U.S. capacity which, according to the Paley Commission report, was not expected to rise above the level of 900,000 tons in the 1950s, rose to nearly 1.3 million tons by 1960.

to projected demand suggested that demand and supply would tend to keep the price of copper within the projected range of 17–24 cents. The ASARCO memoranda also pointed out that, at an estimated operating cost of 12 cents per pound for Toquepala, about half of the world's output was produced at a higher cost than at Toquepala and the other half at a lower cost than at Toquepala. Thus, it was reasoned, Toquepala would have no difficulty keeping competitive with other world producers.

With the rise in copper prices in 1953 and 1954 to 28.8 cents and 29.7 cents, respectively (domestic producers' prices), ASARCO officials adjusted their average price projection from 18.5 cents to 20 cents, but early in 1955—the year the financial arrangements for Toquepala were completed—the U.S. producers' price had risen to 37.5 cents per pound, and the LME price had fallen to 25.8 cents or near the top of the 17–24 cents per pound range in 1952 prices. As will be noted later, it is fortunate that the original 18.5 cents average price projection proved to be far too low, since at that price—even after adjustment for the general rise in world prices—the mine could not have been profitable.

ESTIMATING COSTS AND CAPITAL REQUIREMENTS

The history of the planning and construction of the Toquepala mine illustrates the uncertainties involved in estimating the capital outlays and the operating costs per unit of output. The Toquepala mine, as planned over the period 1952–55, was to be one of the largest mines in the world, and its location, size, and large infrastructure made it difficult to estimate production costs and capital investment. The final cost of the Toquepala mine was nearly 50 percent higher than the original 1952 estimate of $166 million. Moreover, the September 1955 estimate of $205 million also proved to be an underestimate when compared with the actual expenditure of $237 million prior to the beginning of operation in 1960. (The latter amount included capital expenditures of $3.7 million on Cuajone and Quellaveco to that date.) However, the larger outlay may be attributed in part to an increase in annual copper-producing capacity from an estimated 100,000 tons, according to the 1952 plan, to about 140,000 tons, as actually constructed, and also in part to world inflation. Also, the 1955 plan called for mining at a rate of 30,000 tons of ore per day instead of the initial 1952 estimate of 21,600 tons per day, but the actual rate has been somewhat higher than the planned rate of 30,000 tons per day.

Excluding working capital, the original 1952 plan for the Toquepala mine called for an investment of $1,535 per ton of annual capacity. This was found to be somewhat lower than the annual capital outlay per ton for some of the recently constructed mines in the United States. The final capital outlay of $215 million (excluding working capital) represents a capital expenditure of $1,536 per ton on the basis of 140,000 tons of blister copper per year.

The plan for a 30,000 ton-per-day mine adopted in 1954 was estimated to reduce operating costs per pound of refined copper from 11 cents for the first ten years of operation to less than 10 cents. For the second ten years, the operating cost was estimated at 12.4 cents per pound of refined copper, rising to 13.9 cents per pound during the third ten-year period (all in 1954 dollars). The increase reflected the declining grade of the ore to be mined. As has already been noted, product cost during the first two years of operation was actually 9 cents per pound, but by 1972 it had nearly doubled in current dollars and had risen by 50 percent in constant dollars.

PROJECTED PROFITABILITY
OF TOQUEPALA

The uncertainties involved in projecting future copper prices and in estimating capital and operating costs are reflected in the wide disparities in estimates of the profitability of the mine. Given the large capital costs and the high ratio of fixed to variable costs of production, a difference of a few cents per pound in the price of copper can spell the difference between a highly profitable enterprise and one that cannot even meet its annual debt service. This is well illustrated in the profitability estimates made for the Toquepala mine.

In early 1953, under the proposal whereby the ASARCO would finance Toquepala by a $120 million Export–Import Bank loan plus another $10 million or so from suppliers' credits, and on the basis of an equity investment of $48 million, ASARCO officials supplied the Export–Import Bank with projected cash flow estimates based on 18.5 cents-per-pound copper and alternative debt-financing plans. One projection assumed total debt financing of $133.6 million at 5 percent with a maturity of twenty-eight years; a second projection assumed a $132.1 million loan at 4.5 percent with a maturity of twenty-three years; and a third assumed a loan of $130.9 million at 4 percent with a maturity of twenty years. In the projections the expected profits on ASARCO's $48 million investment were given in terms of accounting rates of return averaging from 5.7–5.9 percent for the first ten years of operation and then dropping off sharply under all three assumptions. However, based on the internal rate of return on the ASARCO's investment, the first financing plan yielded a rate of return to the ASARCO on its $48 million investment of less than 1 percent over a twenty-eight-year period; the second and third financing plans yielded negative rates of return over the period equal to the maturities of the loan, that is, the cumulative returns to the ASARCO were less than the $48 million invested.[6]

Considering these low rates of return to the ASARCO on the basis of a projected copper price of 18.5 cents per pound over the periods indicated, one wonders why the company was interested in the mine at all. It seems likely that its decision was made more on the basis of the fact that the Toquepala mine could produce at a cost equal to or lower than nearly half of the output of the world and probably at a cost lower than most of the U.S. copper output. Thus, given the ASARCO's projections of demand and of copper-producing capacity at various copper prices, not only was the company's ability to produce competitively assured, but if the price fell to the point where it was not making a reasonable profit, world output over time would decline relative to demand, and copper prices would rise to a point where profitable production was possible.

The ASARCO's expectation that in the long run copper prices would adjust to cost of production so that a substantial proportion of world output would prove profitable over time was probably a valid one to which greater reliance could be given than to any long-run projection of the price of copper. Also, ASARCO officials may have been influenced by the so-called Notman factor (the ratio of price to production cost), which historically has been estimated at about 1:7. At a production cost of 12 cents per pound (somewhat higher than Toquepala's costs for the first ten years), the long-run price of copper should be slightly in excess of 20 cents per pound. The ASARCO may have also had other motives for investing in Toquepala, namely, the contribution of Toquepala's output to its total operations. Toquepala's initial total output of 100,000 tons per year exceeded ASARCO's existing mine output in the United States and would have provided a dependable source of supply for the company's large refining capacity in the United States.

Assuming an average long-run price of copper of 24 cents per pound,

6 These calculations do not allow for any liquidation value of the mine at the end of the period. But after twenty years the inclusion of liquidation value (usually working capital) would not significantly affect the internal rate of return.

the highest price in ASARCO's projected long-run price range for copper (17–24 cents), the profitability of Toquepala on the basis of the 1953 estimates appears quite favorable. Assuming debt financing of $132.1 million at 4.5 percent and a twenty-three-year repayment period, and taking into account the increased tax payments (but with all of the other assumptions the same as those in ASARCO's initial calculations), an average copper price of 24 cents over the twenty-three-year period would have yielded an internal rate of return of 14.6 percent on ASARCO's $48 million equity investment, as against a negative internal rate of return for 18.5 cents-per-pound copper. This calculation illustrates dramatically the influence of the price assumption for estimating the profitability of a mining venture.

As was discussed in Chapter 1, early in 1954 a new financing plan was formulated for a mine producing at the rate of 30,000 tons of ore per day which required new capital financing totaling $196 million. New equity financing was $80 million, to be supplied by the ASARCO and its prospective partners, in addition to the $10 million in equity financing already invested in Toquepala by the ASARCO. The Export–Import Bank was asked to provide $100 million plus capitalized interest toward the initiation of production, and the remaining $16 million in new financing was to be provided by suppliers' credits and other loans.

In a memorandum prepared by ASARCO officials in May 1954, operating profits (i.e., sales revenues minus production costs) were estimated over a thirty-year period, assuming an average price for copper of 20 cents per pound. For the first ten years of operations, operating profits were estimated at $27.9 million per year; for the second ten years, they were estimated at $15.4 million per year; and for the remaining life of the mine, $9 million per year. Assuming no change in the current (1953) taxes and annual new capital expenditures of $3 million per year, I prepared rough estimates of the net return to the equity stockholders as follows: $10 million per year for the first ten years; $2 million per year for the next five years; and $5 million per year for the remaining fifteen years. Using these estimates, I calculated the internal rate of return on the $90 million in equity investment to be 5.8 percent for the period 1959–88.[7] By current standards such a mine would not be regarded as an attractive investment. However, in 1954 long-term interest rates were less than half

---

[7] I have been informed by an ASARCO official who participated in the investment decision regarding Toquepala that the discounted cash flow (DCF) method of evaluation was not employed in 1953–55; only the accounting rate of return was used with certain adjustments.

the average of those for 1973, and a rate of return of 5.8 percent in 1954 would be equivalent to a 13 or 14 percent rate today. Moreover, in 1954 Peru was regarded as a politically safe area by foreign investors. Account should also be taken of the fact that the ASARCO's long-run strategy was to expand its output of mine copper and to diversify its investments and sources of copper supply geographically.

By the time all of the financing for Toquepala was lined up in September 1955, the outlook for the price of copper must have appeared much more favorable—the 1955 average U.S. producers' price of copper was 37.5 cents per pound. According to working papers in the ASARCO's files, a range of 24–30 cents per pound was being employed in 1955 as the long-run projected price of copper. On the basis of the 1954 estimates of operating profits, and assuming a continuation of the 1954 tax laws, the Toquepala project would have been reasonably profitable producing 24 cents-per-pound copper, and at 30 cents per pound it would have been quite profitable. However, following the construction of the mine there occurred a substantial change in the Peruvian tax laws. Under a law of February 1964, all depletion claimed after 1963 had to be reinvested or else taxed at the going income tax rate. In 1970 the effective tax rate on net earnings paid to Toquepala stockholders was increased from 54.5 to 68 percent. The effects of these changes would have been to reduce substantially the profitability of Toquepala under the 1954 operating profits projection. A rough calculation indicates that the internal rate of return based on the 1954 estimates of the operating profits for 20-cent copper would have been well under 5 percent over the thirty-year period. Fortunately, during the first ten years of operation, operating profit was more than three times the level projected in 1954 despite a sharp rise in operating costs. This made it possible for the company to repay the bulk of the Export–Import Bank loan and all the suppliers' credits, to invest $80 million in Cuajone, and to provide a reasonable rate of return to the stockholders. Beginning with the second half of 1972, all of Toquepala's earnings have been reinvested in Cuajone. The Southern Peru Copper Company's (SPCC) future profitability is in large measure tied to the profitability of the Cuajone mine, which is not expected to begin commercial operations before mid-1976.

4
Contribution of the Toquepala Mine to the Peruvian Economy

Host countries are concerned with several types of economic impacts arising from foreign investments in their mineral industries. These include (1) the expenditures of the mining firms for labor, local materials and equipment, and services within the host country; (2) the contribution to governmental revenues; and (3) the net contribution to national foreign exchange income. The host country is also concerned with less quantifiable economic and social impacts such as the stimulation of the economy through investment in industries supplying the mine (backward integration) and in industries representing forward integration, for example, metal processing and fabrication; the training of labor; the creation of infrastructure that can be used by both the mine and the local economy; and the impact of the mine on the physical environment. A full exploration of the development impacts is beyond the terms of reference of this study. However, an analysis of the allocation of the gross revenues from Toquepala is relevant to the major purpose of this study, namely, the negotiation and operation of mine development agreements. Recently, mine contract negotiations have been concerned not simply with the division of gross operating profits between the government and the foreign investor, but also with employment, training, foreign exchange controls, and forward and backward linkages.

GROSS REVENUES AND RETAINED VALUE

In the following paragraphs we will examine the amount and distribution of gross revenues that are retained in the Peruvian economy, which gives them a direct monetary impact on the economy. Total revenue from Toquepala R, is equal to retained value, RV, plus all external payments. We may express this relationship symbolically as follows:

$$R = RV + M + I + L + P + SE + U$$

where

R = export value f.o.b. (excluding marketing expenses)
RV = retained value
M = imports
I = interest paid on external loans and credits
L = loan repayments
P = profits transferred abroad
SE = salaries of expatriates accruing abroad
U = unidentified items

Retained value, RV, constitutes the sum of all the payments by the Southern Peru Copper Company (SPCC) to the Peruvian economy, and may be expressed as follows:

$$RV = W_n + W_e - SE + DP + T + MD + OT$$

where

W_n = wages and salaries and fringe benefits of Peruvian nationals
W_e = wages and salaries of expatriates
SE = salaries of expatriates accruing abroad
DP = domestic purchases of goods and services
T = income taxes paid to Peruvian government
MD = import duties paid to Peruvian government
OT = other taxes paid to Peruvian government

Table 7 shows the distribution of gross revenues generated by Toquepala over the operating period 1960–72. In the first six years of operations, 1960–65, retained value totaled $134 million, or about 30 percent of gross revenues. Over 60 percent of gross revenues during this period went for imports of materials and equipment required by the mine and for debt service on the loans. Profits transferred abroad constituted only 15 percent of gross revenue. By 1966 the bulk of the loans had been paid off so a larger share of gross revenue became available for profits and taxes. During the 1966–72 period retained value totaled $476 million, or about 49 percent of total gross revenue.[1]

[1] During this period over $78 million of revenues from Toquepala were reinvested in Cuajone. A portion of the expenditures on Cuajone also constitute retained value, and some of these expenditures are included in the data given in Tables 7 and 8.

Table 7. Distribution of Toquepala Gross Revenue, 1960–72
(millions of U.S. dollars)

	1960–65	1966–72	1960–72
1. Gross revenue (R)	450.0	970.7	1,420.7
2. Retained value (RV)[a]	133.5	476.1	609.6
3. Imports (M)	77.9	68.1	146.0
4. Interest on loans (I)	24.2	3.5	27.7
5. Loan repayments (L)[b]	175.1	26.5	201.6
6. Salaries of expatriates transferred abroad (SE)	6.6	8.7	15.3
7. Profits transferred abroad (P)	69.1	220.8	289.9
8. Reinvested in Cuajone	1.6	78.4	80.0
9. Sum of items 2 through 8	488.0	882.1	1,370.1
10. Unidentified items and statistical discrepancy (U) (1 minus 9)[c]	−38.0	88.6	50.6

[a] See Table 8.
[b] Includes Export–Import Bank loan, suppliers' credits, and advances by partners.
[c] Includes depreciation transferred abroad.

It should also be mentioned that a substantial portion of the $227 million spent during the exploration and construction period prior to 1960 represented payments to the Peruvian economy in the form of payrolls and domestic purchases of materials, equipment, and services. Data on these outlays are not available to the author.

During the 1966–72 period profits transferred abroad represented about 23 percent of total gross revenue. However, for the entire twelve-year period, 1960–72, profits transferred abroad represented only 20 percent of total gross revenues. Of the total $1,421 million in gross revenue obtained over the 1960–72 period, about 43 percent constituted retained value, 26 percent represented external payments for imports and debt service, 20 percent was accounted for by profits transferred abroad, about 5 percent was reinvested in Cuajone, and 2 percent represented other amounts transferred abroad.

Table 8 shows the distribution of retained value generated by the Toquepala mine over the 1960–72 period. During the first six years of operations (1960–65), income taxes, import duties, and other taxes represented about 44 percent of total retained value of $134 million; the remainder was divided between wages and salaries ($39 million) and domestic purchases ($46 million). Over the period 1966–72, retained value totaled $476 million, of which over 58 percent constituted income taxes, import duties, and other taxes, with the remainder going to wages and salaries and the Mining Community ($96 million), and to domestic purchases of materials and services ($102 million). Over the thirteen-year period 1960–72, out of $610 million in retained

Table 8. Distribution of Retained Value Generated by Toquepala, 1960–72
(millions of U.S. dollars)

	1960–65	1966–72	1960–72
Retained value (RV)	133.5	476.1	609.6
Wages and salaries of nationals (W_n)	32.4	78.8	111.2
Wages and salaries of expatriates			
not transferred abroad ($W_e - SE$)	7.0	8.4	15.4
Domestic purchases of materials			
and services (DP)	46.3	102.2	148.5
Income taxes (T)	29.9	232.3	262.2
Import duties (MD)	12.3	24.6	36.9
Other taxes (OT)	5.6	21.0	26.6
Provision for Mining Community			
and Institute (MC)[a]	—	8.8	8.8

[a] Includes provision for equity participation.

value, 53 percent went to government, 21 percent to labor, 24 percent to domestic purchases of materials and services, and about 1 percent to the Mining Community.

Beyond 1972 retained value—as a percentage of total revenue—will probably rise, and profits—as a percentage of gross revenues—will decline. Depreciation decreases sharply after 1975, thereby raising taxable income, which is subject to a 68 percent tax. Imports for Toquepala have declined while expenditures in Peru for goods and services are rising rapidly. Wage payments have been rising at over 20 percent per year, although employment in Toquepala has stabilized at 3,870 employees. In addition, a substantial amount of revenue will be paid to the Mining Community.

The Sharing of Before-Tax Earnings

Host countries tend to be concerned with their share of before-tax earnings after allowance for capital consumption. The item in Table 7, "profits transferred abroad," is the same as earnings after Peruvian taxes of the majority stockholders (excluding earnings on equity held by the Mining Community). For the entire period 1960–72, the SPCC's earnings totaled $290 million after taxes, while Peruvian income taxes over the same period totaled $262 million. This means that 52 percent of before-tax earnings went to the company and 48 percent went to the government. However, for the period 1966–72, 54 percent of before-tax earnings went to the government and the government's share increased steadily after 1968; in 1972 it was in excess of 60 percent.

It should be noted that there are difficulties in comparing the relative shares of the rents accruing to the government with those of the foreign stockholders on the basis of the division of before-tax earnings. During the first six years of the Toquepala mine operation, no dividends were paid to the stockholders. During this period nearly all the depreciation, amortization, and depletion, plus the after-tax earnings, were required for debt retirement (including repayment of stockholders' advances), capital expenditures on Toquepala, and additions to working capital. Over the 1966–72 period, the SPCC paid $277 million in dividends to stockholders, somewhat less than the $290 million in after-tax earnings during the entire period 1960–72. Dividends could have been higher during the 1966–72 period had not a portion of the depletion allowance been invested in Cuajone; stockholders sacrificed dividends in order to acquire an equity interest in the new mine. There is also the question of whether depletion should be regarded as capital consumption—since depreciation and amortization allowances provided for the full recovery of capital outlays on Toquepala—or as an incentive to investment. This question is complicated by the fact that depreciation never provides sufficient funds for replacement of worn-out equipment when it must be replaced at substantially higher prices; nor does it cover certain additional capital expenditures that must be made during the production period in order to maintain output. These questions will be dealt with in Chapter 5, in which we analyze the financial operations of the SPCC.

OTHER IMPACTS ON THE PERUVIAN ECONOMY

Foreign Exchange Impact

The gross foreign exchange contribution to the Peruvian economy is the same as retained value. However, goods and services purchased by the SPCC in the national economy have a substantial import content, probably well in excess of the 11 percent ratio of total Peruvian imports to the GNP. The import content of the local purchases of goods and services by employees of the mine is also likely to be higher than the national average. Nevertheless, 90 percent or more of retained value constitutes net foreign exchange.

Impact on Employment

The number of people on the payroll of the SPCC has remained quite stable throughout the 1960–72 period. At the end of 1960 there were 3,855 persons on the payroll; this number rose to a high of 3,939 at the end of 1964, and was 3,870 at the end of both 1971 and 1972. The number of salaried employees (those paid monthly) has been rising steadily from a low of 573 at the end of 1960 to a high of 904 at the end of 1972. The number of expatriates has declined significantly over the period, decreasing from 242 at the end of 1960 to 133 at the end of 1972 (3.4 percent of the work force). Total payroll payments to Peruvian nationals have risen sharply over the period from $3.7 million during 1960 to $18.3 million during 1972. During this same period, total payroll payments to expatriate employees rose from $2.6 million to $3.1 million.

Expenditures for Peruvian Goods and Services

Expenditures by the SPCC for Peruvian goods and services have risen from $5.9 million in 1960 to $22.9 million in 1972. On the other hand, imports by the company have declined from a high of $16.7 million in 1960 to $5.1 million in 1972. I was unable to obtain information regarding the composition of either the imports or the goods and services purchased in the local economy. However, SPCC officials' have stated that the increase in local purchases is mainly a consequence of the growth in the variety and quality of Peruvian products, the production of some of which has been directly sponsored by the SPCC.

The Resource Impact

One of the difficulties with the retained value approach to measuring the impact of a foreign investment on the national economy is that it disregards the fact that the country has obtained a valuable mine. Retained value is a flow concept, but it should be emphasized that creation of the Toquepala mine has made a contribution to the productive assets of the nation, together with a highway, a railroad, a port, and other infrastructure that serve the community as well as the mine. Although the foreign suppliers of capital have certain claims on the revenues of the mine, including the repayment of borrowed capital, the mine will remain as an income-earning asset long after the loan capital has been repaid—and the capital supplied by the owners of the foreign equity has been amortized. Except for a reasonable rate of return on foreign equity (half of which will eventually be owned by nationals under the Mining Community regime), the mine and its revenue belong to the nation.

5
Financial Analysis
of Toquepala

RETURNS TO ORIGINAL
STOCKHOLDERS

The purpose of this chapter is to analyze the financial returns from Toquepala to the original stockholders of the Southern Peru Copper Company (SPCC). In addition to the $32.6 million invested in equity, the stockholders made advances totaling $74.8 million during the construction period. The advances were made without interest and should be regarded as risk capital for purposes of calculating the internal rate of return to stockholders' investment. No dividends were paid for the first six years of mine operations. Beginning with 1961, the SPCC made repayments on the stockholders' advances, and by 1966 the full $74.8 million had been repaid. As was noted in Chapter 2, prior to 1966 all of the cash flow from depreciation, amortization, depletion, and after-tax earnings were required to repay the Export–Import Bank loan, the suppliers' credits, and the stockholders' advances, plus the required investment in Toquepala. In addition, about $1.5 million was invested in Cuajone and Quellaveco during this period. Investment in Cuajone rose from about $1.5 million per year over the 1965–67 period to $3.1 million and $3.7 million, respectively, in 1968 and 1969. Investment in Cuajone then rose sharply to $13.6 million in 1970, $18 million in 1971, and $37 million in 1972. This investment was not required to maintain output in Toquepala but rather constituted reinvestment of cash flow in a new mine in which SPCC stockholders were accumulating equity. The bulk of the investment in Cuajone was financed by the depletion allowance from Toquepala. Had the SPCC elected to pay the depletion allowance in dividends to its stockholders, it would have been taxed at rates ranging from 54.5 to 68 percent. Hence, in calculating the cash flow to the SPCC stockholders, I have included the amounts invested in Cuajone less the tax that would have been paid had these amounts been paid out in dividends.

Table 9 shows the cash outflow supplied by the SPCC stockholders (including the $74.8 million in advances) during the construction period, and the net cash flow (NCF) to stockholders over the period 1960–72. NCF during the production period includes repayment of stockholders' advances, dividends, and amounts reinvested in Cuajone less taxes on depletion that would have been paid had the depletion been paid out in dividends.[1] Over the thirteen-year period 1960–72, the internal rate of return to the SPCC stockholders was 13.5 percent (see Table 9). If we add to the final year a liquidation value equal to the difference between current assets and current liabilities of the SPCC at the end of 1972 (or $53 million), we obtain an internal rate of return of 13.6 percent for the thirteen-year period. However, in constant (1972) prices the internal rate of return is 12.3 percent.[2]

Although an internal rate of return calculation assumes that there will be no further NCF to the investor beyond the final year of the period for which the calculation is made, extending the period of NCF beyond, say, twenty years, makes little difference in the calculated rate of return. If we project a constant annual NCF equal to the average NCF to SPCC stockholders for 1971 and 1972, for an additional seven years beyond 1972, the internal rate of return for the twenty-year period, including a $53 million liquidation value, is 15.3 percent.[3] If we were to assume that this same NCF continued for an additional ten years to 1989, the internal rate of return for the entire thirty-year period would increase by less than one-half of 1 percent over the internal rate of return for the twenty-year period.

The internal rate of return over a twenty-year period, as calculated above, is based on NCF to stockholders during 1971 and 1972 extrapolated to the seven-year period 1973–79. In the light of the 1973 surge in the price of copper (followed by the sharp decline in 1974), this calculation might be regarded as highly unrealistic. Nevertheless, it is not likely that the internal rate of return for the full

---

[1] A portion of the depletion during this period was reinvested in Toquepala and hence not subject to taxation. These amounts were not included in NCF to stockholders. No account was taken of U.S. government intercompany taxes on dividends paid by the SPCC to its stockholders.

[2] Both cash outflow and inflow deflated by the 1972 U.S. wholesale price index.

[3] If we use constant (1972) prices, the internal rate of return is 14 percent.

Table 9. Toquepala: Cash Flow to Majority Equity Stockholders and Internal Rates of Return (IRR), 1941–79

Exploration–construction period		Production period		1973–1979 projection[a]	
Year	Cash flow to stockholders	Year	Cash flow to stockholders	Year	Based on average of 1971–72 cash flow
1941–54	(12.4)	1961	14.4	1973	40.1
1955	(1.5)	1962	13.5	1974	40.1
1956	(31.0)	1963	16.1	1975	40.1
1957	(29.0)	1964	15.7	1976	40.1
1958	(19.5)	1965	15.4	1977	40.1
1959	(14.0)	1966	41.9	1978	40.1
1960	0	1967	46.5	1979	40.1
		1968	43.5		
		1969	55.0		
		1970	45.1		
		1971	37.5		
		1972	42.7		
IRR for 1941–72 = 0.136				IRR for 1941–79 = 0.153	

Note: Numbers in parentheses indicate outflow in millions of U.S. dollars. Liquidation value for 1979 is 53.0.
[a] For the years 1973–79, cash flow can also be projected at a rate 50 percent higher than average for 1971–72, or as 60.2.

twenty-year period would be substantially higher. Before reaching this conclusion, however, we must examine the composition of future cash flow. Amortization of the mine development expenditures terminated in 1972 and after 1975 depreciation and depletion on the original investment will decline substantially. During the three-year period 1970–72, these allowances generated over half the NCF to Toquepala shareholders. Although copper prices are likely to remain substantially higher than they were in 1972, the continuation of a London Metal Exchange (LME) price of well above a dollar a pound over the next few years is regarded as unlikely. Meanwhile costs are increasing rapidly, and the Mining Communities' proprietary participation on an ever-increasing basis will reduce cash flow to the original stockholders. Finally, an increase in the NCF in the later years of the twenty-year period is heavily discounted in the calculation of the internal rate of return. To illustrate this point, let us assume that for the 1973–75 period NCF is 50 percent higher than what was projected for the same period in our initial calculation, but that after 1975 NCF declines to the level of the initial projection (see Table 9). Under these assumptions the internal rate of return for the full twenty-year period 1960–79 is 15.7[4] as compared with 15.3 for the initial calculation.

The Accounting Rate of Return

The accounting rate of return, while perhaps the most popular measure of profitability, has the major weakness of not taking into account the time pattern relating to both investment expenditures and returns. A common method is to calculate the ratio of after-tax earnings to the net book value of assets. The net book value of assets is equal to the value of fixed assets at cost minus accumulated depreciation, depletion, and amortization, plus the excess of current and miscellaneous (nonfixed) assets over current and long-term liabilities. On this basis, net book value is equal to stockholders' equity. Total investment in Toquepala prior to the beginning of operations in 1960 was $233 million (including $18.7 million in working capital). Subsequent investments in Toquepala totaled $45 million plus an investment of $83 million in Cuajone, reaching a total of $361 million as the gross book value of assets at the end of 1972. However, over the 1960–72 period aggregate depreciation, depletion, and amortization for Toquepala was (by coincidence) $361 million. Hence there is no net asset basis for calculating the accounting rate of return as the ratio of after-tax earnings to net book value.

[4] If we use constant (1972) prices, the internal rate of return is 14.4 percent.

Since the SPCC has recovered its invested capital, is it entitled to a return on its investment? And, if so, how should that return be determined? These questions point up a serious difficulty with the accounting rate of return: it fails to consider the fact that the equity investors received no dividends during the construction period nor during the first six years of productive operations; nor did they receive any interest on the $75 million in stockholders' advances.

Book value as a basis for determining the rate of return also has the disadvantage of not allowing for the effects of inflation, both within the host country and worldwide. A better basis for asset evaluation is replacement value minus observed depreciation. An independent appraisal of the present-day cost of the physical properties at Toquepala provided an estimate of $347 million, as of the end of 1970.[5] This figure does not include the value of working capital at the end of 1970, the cost of the mineral land, or the amortized expenditures for premine stripping. Observed depreciation of the physical properties was established at $103 million, giving a value of the physical properties at present-day cost minus depreciation of $244 million at the end of 1970. Taking account of the increase in prices since 1970, together with $5 million in additional investment in Toquepala during 1971–72, it would not appear inappropriate to assume the same net asset value for 1972, as was established at the end of 1970. If we add to this amount $30 million in current and miscellaneous assets minus liabilities at the end of 1972 plus the $10 million cost of mineral lands and $30 million in expenditures for premine stripping (not included in the above appraisal), we arrive at a figure of $314 million as a conservative estimate of the net replacement value of Toquepala and of stockholders' equity. If to this amount we add $83 million in the SPCC stockholders' equity in Cuajone at the end of 1972, the total for both properties is $397 million. However, in order to determine the accounting rate of return over the entire period of 1960–72 as the ratio of after-tax earnings to net replacement value, it would be necessary to recalculate net replacement value for each year. We may also question the appropriateness of using after-tax earnings as the numerator in the calculation of the accounting rate of return. A more appropriate figure might be NCF, as defined on page 6. Using NCF as the numerator and net replacement value of assets in Toquepala alone as the denominator, the accounting rate of return was 13.6 percent in 1972 and 11.9 percent in 1971. Using the same asset value as the denominator and average NCF to stockholders for the five-year period 1968–72 as the

[5] The appraisal was made by the firm Ford, Bacon and Davis, Inc., New York City.

numerator, the accounting rate of return is 14.2 percent.[6] If we use the value of assets in both Toquepala and Cuajone at the end of 1972, the accounting rate of return for that year is 10.8 percent; and using average cash flow for the period 1968–72, the accounting rate of return is 11.3 percent.

Although the accounting rate of return cannot be justified as a basis for measuring the rate of profits on stockholders' equity, regardless of what adjustments are made in the concept, the purpose of the above analysis is to show that with appropriate adjustments the accounting rate of return may turn out to be equal to or less than the internal rate of return. However, when the accounting rate of return is calculated as the ratio of after-tax earnings to net book value, it may prove to be extremely high and bear no relationship to the internal rate of return.

[6] Had after-tax earnings rather than NCF been employed, the accounting rates of return calculated above would have been much lower, since NCF includes amortization, dividends, depletion, and depreciation not reinvested in Toquepala, minus taxes on depletion not reinvested in Toquepala.

6
A Brief History
of the
Bougainville Mine

DISCOVERY AND EXPLORATION

The subject of this case study is located on the island of Bougainville, which forms a part of the self-governing territory of Papua New Guinea (PNG). Bougainville is about 130 miles long and 30 miles wide and lies over 600 miles from the main island of New Guinea. (Geographically Bougainville is a part of the Solomon Islands chain.) For several decades a German colony, Bougainville became part of the Australian Mandate at the end of World War II and later became a part of the Australian Territory of Papua New Guinea (PNG), which obtained self-governing status in December 1973.

Although the Panguna area of Bougainville island had been known to contain some copper since the 1930s—it had been worked for gold between 1930–51—the actual discovery of the porphyry copper deposit was made in the spring of 1964 by a group of geologists employed by the Conzinc Riotinto of Australia Ltd. (CRA). Following a preliminary examination that showed the deposit to be promising, there followed several years of extensive drilling, metallurgical testing, and evaluation. The evaluation, which was not completed until mid-1969, has been described in mining journals as one of the most thorough and sophisticated ever carried out for an open-pit mine.[1]

---

[1] A description of the evaluation is given by M. R. L. Blackwell, chief mining engineer, Bougainville Copper Pty. Ltd., in two articles: "Some Aspects of the Evaluation and Planning of the Bougainville Copper Project," in *Decision Making in the Mineral Industry*, special vol. 12 (Montreal: The Canadian Institute of Mining and Metallurgy, 1971); and "A Model of Bougainville Copper's Panguna Ore Body," in M. D. G. Solomon and F. H. Lancaster, eds., *Application of Computer Methods in the Mineral Industry* (Johannesburg: The South African Institute of Mining and Metallurgy, 1973).

The Bougainville ore body consists of 900 million metric tons of ore with an average grade of 0.48 percent copper and 0.55 gm (0.018 troy ounces) of gold per ton. For every 1,000 pounds of copper metal produced, about 1.7 troy ounces of gold and 3.5 ounces of silver are recovered. Because of the low grade of the ore body, it was found necessary to mine and process ore on a scale never before realized— some 90,000 tons per day—in order to make the operation profitable. According to an article in the *Engineering and Mining Journal*, the Bougainville mine is "the largest first-stage copper operation ever conceived, designed and developed to date."[2] The physical and social environment in which the mine is located presented challenging problems for both the exploration and the development of the mine. The open-pit mine is located at the 3,000-foot level in a remote jungle-covered island untouched by industry and without an industrial labor force. A mountain road crossing a 3,500-foot pass had to be created, together with facilities for mining communities which attained a maximum population of over 10,000 people in the construction period.

The expenditures for exploration and evaluation of the deposit, which totaled over A$21 million before the final decision was made to develop the mine, were shared by CRA and New Broken Hill Consolidated Ltd. (NBHC).[3] In June 1967 the Bougainville Copper Pty. Ltd. (BCPL) was formed; it was owned two-thirds by CRA and one-third by NBHC, and incorporated within PNG. By mid-1967 the promoters of the Bougainville mine concluded that their deposit was highly promising, but before spending another A$10 million or so on the evaluation of the mine and before attempting to raise the large amount of capital required for its construction, they deemed it necessary to negotiate a mining agreement with the administration of the Territory of PNG (hereafter it will be referred to as the administration). The agreement was negotiated with officials of the Australian government in consultation with local PNG politicians and was approved by the PNG House of Assembly in October 1967.

---

[2] "Bougainville: The New Face in Copper Mining," *Engineering and Mining Journal* (February 1973), pp. 63–64.

[3] CRA is a subsidiary of Rio Tinto–Zinc Corporation of the United Kingdom. NBHC is a holding company with mining properties in Australia, and CRA has an equity interest in NBHC. NBHC was dissolved in 1973, and its shares in Bougainville Mining Ltd. (BML) were distributed to the NBHC stockholders. BML held 80 percent of the shares of BCPL with the remaining BCPL shares held by the PNG government.

THE BOUGAINVILLE COPPER
PROJECT (BCP) AGREEMENT

The negotiation of the BCP mine development agreement[4] must be considered in the context of the political and economic environment of PNG in 1967. Although PNG had a legislative body, the House of Assembly, elected by popular vote, the responsibility for negotiating the agreement for large-scale development of natural resources was with the Australian government's minister of external territories. In 1969 the political independence of PNG, even the domestic self-government status achieved in December 1973,[5] was not contemplated for at least another ten years. Hence it was expected that Australia would continue to subsidize the PNG budget and provide various forms of developmental assistance. Nevertheless, the Australian government was anxious to promote PNG's financial independence, and in particular to promote a mineral industry that would expand PNG's exports, since the economy had a substantial external deficit.

In view of emerging independence for PNG, the Australian government recognized the importance of negotiating an agreement with the Australian mining firm that would win approval by a large majority of the PNG House of Assembly and the support of the public generally, especially the people of Bougainville. At the time CRA began prospecting in Bougainville, PNG mining ordinances had no special provision for dealing with projects of such a scale and nature. In fact, under the then-existing legislation, BCP might have expected to obtain a mining lease on request once it had proved up the deposit. Under existing tax legislation, the company tax was only 20 percent, and in addition, since the project was of a pioneering nature, the company might have expected to qualify for a five-year tax exemption under the terms of PNG's pioneer industry legislation.[6] However, in 1966, following initial discussions regarding the issuance of mining leases for the development of the Panguna deposit, PNG's mining ordinances were amended so as to secure flexibility for the negotiation of special mining contracts for large-scale operations. One of the provisions of

[4] Ordinance No. 70, 1967, Territory of Papua New Guinea, October 1967.

[5] Australia still controls PNG's external relations. However, the PNG government has full autonomy with respect to the regulation of foreign investment, including the right to alter contracts negotiated by the Australian government prior to self-government. In any case, full independence is expected to be granted sometime in 1975.

[6] See G. O. Gutman, "Objectives, Strategy and Tactics in Mining Projects with Reference to Bougainville Copper," a paper presented at the Seventh Waigani Seminar on Law and Development in Melanesia, Port Moresby, April 1973, p. 21.

the new legislation—requested by Paul Lapun, a House of Assembly member from Bougainville—was the apportionment of 5 percent of the royalties from mining operations to local landowners. The new legislation also established provision for compensation for damage to local landowners and occupation fees to be paid to the landowners.[7] The new legislation also made it possible to negotiate tax arrangements which could be more liberal to the private company with respect to certain provisions than those provided under the general mining laws, while at the same time providing higher tax rates than those allowed under the general mining law.

It seems likely that when CRA obtained a special prospecting authority for exploring Bougainville island in December 1963, the company gave little thought to a future mine development agreement, since under existing law (which was patterned after Australian mining and tax legislation) it was entitled to obtain a mining lease more or less automatically once it had proved the deposit, with provisions in accordance with the general tax and other stipulations in existing legislation. But after having spent several million dollars in exploration and evaluation, and in the light of the PNG independence movement, the company became anxious to negotiate a development contract before making larger outlays. From the beginning of its activities there was substantial opposition on Bougainville island by those natives living close to the exploration areas who resented the intrusion of foreign workers (including those from other parts of PNG) upon their land, fearing the potential damage to their environment and their traditional way of life. Hence, both the company and the Australian government were anxious to negotiate an agreement that would have the support of the majority of the local electorate in Bougainville and in PNG generally.

In approaching the mining agreement negotiations CRA had two major concerns. First, the Bougainville mine was to be a very large operation requiring substantial amounts of borrowed capital repayable within seven or eight years after the beginning of operations. CRA wanted low or no taxes (other than royalties) during the period of debt repayment. A tax rate of 40–50 percent on earnings from the beginning of operation (in terms of 1967 price expectations) meant that all of their cash flow would have been absorbed by debt repayment and additional capital expenditures. Moreover, the external creditors usually demand that provision is made for a substantial margin of cash flow above debt service. The company's second concern was

---

[7] See Commonwealth of Australia, *Papua New Guinea Report for 1970–1971* (Canberra: Commonwealth of Australia, 1972), pp. 105–106.

with the political risk involved. In view of the fact that the mine was to cost A$100 million—and it actually cost about A$400 million—and that much of this would have to be borrowed, the company sought some assurance against expropriation by a future independent PNG government. However, such an assurance was not forthcoming from the Australian government, even though there is a government organization that insures foreign investment. It is quite likely that CRA would have pressed its demand, perhaps even to the point of refusing to make the investment, had it realized that PNG would become self-governing by 1973. The Australian government rejected this demand and suggested that such action would imply a lack of faith on its part in any future independent government of PNG. The agreement did provide, however, that BCPL would be free from interference in its legitimate operations under the agreement and from the expropriation of its properties or leases; that the shareholders would be permitted to enjoy the benefits of their equity holdings without impairment; and that the company would be free to declare and pay dividends. However, the agreement is between BCPL and the administration of the Territory of PNG and the independent government of PNG has the sovereign right to change the agreement in any respect.

The following paragraphs describe briefly the major provisions of the 1967 agreement that are of special interest for purposes of this study.

Leases and Royalties

During the period through September 30, 1971, the company could apply for mining leases over the whole or part of the area of PNG, subject to its prospecting authority for use in mining operations, and for plants, transportation, wharves, disposal of overburden and tailings, and other purposes required by the mine. On the receipt of such leases the company agreed to spend at least A$30 million for the construction of the mine and installations within five years of its being granted the leases. Initially, the leases were for forty-two years, with successive rights of renewal for further terms of twenty-one years. For the first forty-two years, a rental for mining leases was set for A$1 per acre per annum and royalties at 1.25 percent of the f.o.b. value of the ore concentrates sales, with the right of renewal on these same terms for two additional twenty-one-year periods. In addition to these amounts paid to the administration, BCPL was to pay the owners of the land an occupation fee of A$2 per acre per annum, or 5 percent of the unimproved capital value, whichever was the larger. It may be noted that the company did not make a final decision to construct the mine until it had completed its evaluation, had negotiated long-term contracts for the copper concentrate, and had arranged for the loan financing.

Government Equity Participation

The administration was offered the right to purchase 20 percent of BCPL's ordinary share capital at par. Not later than two years after the granting of the special mining leases the company was required to notify the administration of the total amount of its share of capital, and not later than six months thereafter the administration could determine whether to accept the offer. The administration retained the right to transfer a portion, not to exceed 25 percent, of its shareholding to Territory residents. So long as the administration holds at least 15 percent of the share capital of the company, it is entitled to appoint a director of the company.

Import Duties

The agreement provides that no import duties or other levies shall be imposed on the importation of plant equipment, vehicles, fuels, and other supplies required for the construction of the mine and its installations and infrastructure or for the replacement of any plant machinery or equipment for ten years after the completion of the mine. There is, however, the further provision that the exemption from duties shall not apply to any equipment or materials available in the Territory at reasonable prices.

Taxation

The basic law governing the taxation of mining companies in PNG at the time of negotiations was the Income Tax Ordinance 1959–70 of Papua New Guinea. (This law followed closely the Income Tax Assessment Act 1936–67 of the Commonwealth of Australia.) The taxation provisions of the BCP agreement refer to sections of this act and are in accord with it except for certain special tax arrangements that apply specifically to BCPL. Moreover, those sections of the Income Tax Ordinance 1959–70 that apply to BCPL continue to apply, even if the relevant provisions of the ordinance should be changed. For example, Section 33 of that ordinance, which exempts from taxation 20 percent of the income from the production of certain minerals, including copper, has been eliminated from the ordinance but remains in force for BCPL. The following are the major tax provisions that apply to BCP for the life of the agreement:

1. There is a tax holiday with respect to the company income tax for the first three years of operations.

2. At the end of the tax holiday the company may deduct capital expenditures for mine preparation, plant and equipment, and outlays for purposes relating to the construction of the mine in the calculation of taxable income for as many years as may be necessary for the full recovery of the capital outlays. (This provision is referred to in the agreement as Division 10 of the Income Tax Ordinance 1959–70.)

3. Twenty percent of taxable income of BCPL is exempt from income taxation.

4. During the first year that BCPL has a taxable income, that is, following the tax holiday and the Division 10 rapid depreciation deductions, the tax rate will be the regular PNG company tax rate (currently 25 percent). Thereafter the tax rate increases in annual steps until the fifth year when it rises to 50 percent or to an effective rate of 40 percent after the deduction of 20 percent of taxable income, referred to in paragraph 3 above.

5. The 50 percent rate of tax on taxable income continues until the twenty-sixth year of production when the rate rises by 1 percent in each of the following years until it reaches a maximum of 66 percent.

6. There is a 15 percent tax on all dividends transferred to non-residents of PNG.[8]

The tax regime was the subject of considerable bargaining between administration and BCP officials. The company was able to convince the administration that, because of the large debt-service payments during the first seven or eight years of operation, no income tax obligation should exist. Under the company's assumptions regarding future copper prices and revenues in 1967, the combination of the tax holiday and the Division 10 rapid depreciation allowance in effect consecutively virtually assured a seven-year period during which there would be no taxable income. It was also expected that during this period dividends would be low or nonexistent, since nearly all the cash flow would be devoted to debt retirement and the accumulation of a cash reserve. During this period, therefore, the PNG government's income from mining operations (excluding taxation of mine employees) would be limited to the 1.25 percent royalty payment (less 5 percent of the royalties to be paid to the landowners in Bougainville).

The company sought as a package a total ceiling on payments made

[8] The tax arrangements are discussed in greater detail in Chapter 8.

to cover the company tax, royalties, tariffs, and other charges amounting to 50 percent of taxable income before applying the 20 percent
exemption of company income from taxation. The administration
agreed to the 50 percent ceiling but with the royalty to be excluded
from this limit. For an analysis of the company's expected rate of
return on the investment, see Chapter 7.

Government Investment Undertakings

Unlike some agreements which obligate the foreign investor to provide
all of the infrastructure and many of the public services relating to the
mining community, under the BCP agreement the administration
reserved for itself the right to provide education, police, postal, telecommunications, and medical facilities to serve the company, its
employees, and the new communities on Bougainville island which
arose as a consequence of the mine. Among the government's projects
were the upgrading of certain roads, communications, power trans-
mission lines, and infrastructure required for education, health, and
law and order. The value of these capital outlays has been estimated at
A$41 million over the period 1969–70/1974–75. About half the outlays
are financed by an A$20 million loan from the Australian government,
repayable at 6⅔ percent interest over the period 1974–84.

Steep terrain restricted the mountain township of Panguna, a company
responsibility, so much that another area was needed to house the
employees. The administration decided that a large expatriate plantation on the coast at Arawa was the most suitable area for a larger
town to be developed jointly by the administration and the company.
This new town would serve not simply as a mine dormitory but as the
administrative center for the whole of the island. There are also
economic advantages to this plan that tend to offset the additional
financial burden on the public treasury. First, had the company provided the investment, the interest cost would have been higher, and
interest is deductible when calculating taxable income. In addition,
under the provisions of the BCP agreement, capital outlays can be
written off in calculating taxable income. Hence, had BCPL made the
investment, the time when the PNG government received income tax
revenues from the company would have been further delayed. Finally,
had BCPL been required to provide the investment expenditures, the
company would undoubtedly have demanded a more liberal tax
arrangement since its debt service would have been higher, and hence
earnings to equity stockholders would have been lower or further
deferred until after the debt had been liquidated. Since the Australian

government provided half of the funds for the investment by means of a low-interest loan with a maturity in excess of twenty years, it can readily be shown that the PNG government is better off for having assumed the investment obligation.

Provisions Relating to the Bougainvillians

PNG is an amalgam of several territories containing different ethnic populations with separate political and social histories, and Bougainville was perhaps the least integrated of these territories. The Bougainvillians felt that the owners of the land on which the mine was to be situated were entitled to royalty payments for minerals taken from the land, or if the royalty payments were to be made to the government, they should be made to the local government of Bougainville. However, under Australian law (and hence under PNG law) mineral rights to the land were vested in the Crown and royalties were to be paid to the Territorial administration and, after independence, to the government of PNG.

Altogether the total area required by BCPL was about 60 square miles, approximately 0.8 percent of the area of Bougainville island, or 0.02 percent of the total area of PNG. Seventy percent of the occupied area is required for the disposal of tailing. For an annual rental of A$1 per acre, the company acquired leases on the land covered by the special mining lease as well as on lands outside the original prospecting area for infrastructure and other purposes. In addition to paying the government rental for the mineral rights plus a royalty of 1.25 percent of the value of the metal output, it was necessary for the company to pay annual rentals and cash compensation to the local owners of the land, both for its use and for any destruction and damage to crops, gardens, and fishing grounds, and for village resettlement, including replanting of crops. The amounts to be paid by the company to the Bougainvillians were not spelled out in the agreement, but the government fixed occupation fees at A$2 per acre, or 5 percent, of the unproved value of the land, whichever is greater. Compensation for the destruction of cacao and coffee plants was determined by negotiation and later in some cases by litigation, all of which has resulted in considerable expense to the company. In retrospect, it might have been better for the government to have handled these matters directly and given the company the right to use land without having to settle with the local landowners. On the other hand, the landowners probably got a better deal from the company than they would have gotten from the government. For a discussion of payments to the local landowners, see Chapter 8.

Local Purchases and the Hiring and Training of Local Personnel

The BCP agreement states that the company shall, so far as practicable, use supplies, machinery, and equipment manufactured or produced in the Territory. However, virtually none of the plant equipment and vehicles and very few of the materials required by the mine are, in fact, produced in PNG.

The BCP agreement also provides that the company shall, so far as is reasonable and practicable, "use and train in new skills labor available in the Territory and in particular the Company shall continue and expand the training program instituted prior to the execution hereof with a view to the early employment by it in technical and staff positions of suitably qualified inhabitants of the Territory." Although some Papua New Guineans have criticized the agreement for not specifying local employment targets, the company has endeavored to carry out the provisions of the agreement by means of its training and expatriate replacement program. (See Chapter 8, for a more complete discussion of this program.)

Processing the Ore

The question of establishing a smelter and possibly a refinery was discussed in some detail between the administration and BCP at the time of the contract negotiations. The administration was concerned on the one hand with the contribution of processing to the industrial development of the Territory and with the adverse ecological consequences on the other. The company did not want to establish processing facilities at the time: first, because it wanted to negotiate long-term contracts for concentrates; and second, because it did not want to increase the already high investment requirement for the development of the mine. Hence, the agreement simply permits the company to submit plans for processing at a later date. However, both the company and the PNG government believe that there is a strong moral obligation to give consideration to processing sometime in the future.

Expropriation and Arbitration

The BCP agreement contains a clause designed to protect the company against interference with its operations consistent with the provisions of the agreement, discriminatory fiscal or social legislation, and cancellation of leases or expropriation of assets. According to the agreement, expropriation includes "any substantial interference of the rights of the owner fully to utilize, to enjoy or to deal with or dispose of the assets, product or share and in the case of a business, any substantial interference with the rights of the owner to control or carry on or to deal with or dispose of that business. . . ."

The BCP agreement also provides for the arbitration of disputes with each side entitled to appoint one arbitrator; in the event a third arbitrator cannot be agreed upon by the parties, he shall be appointed by the president of the International Chamber of Commerce.

While the above provisions are clearly binding on the Australian government as administrator of the Territory, they could be changed by the PNG government now that it has achieved self-governing status.

RENEGOTIATION OF THE BCP AGREEMENT IN 1974

As described in Chapter 10, the BCP agreement was substantially changed in the course of renegotiation over the period April–October 1974. The major change was in the tax arrangement. Under the new tax regime, retroactive to January 1, 1974, the company will pay taxes at a rate of $33\frac{1}{3}$ percent on net earnings up to A$86 million and 70 percent on earnings in excess of this amount. The financial impact on the company is substantial, since it gives up both accelerated depreciation and the tax holiday and becomes subject to an increased tax rate as well. An evaluation of the impact on the new tax regime is presented in Chapter 9.

CAPITAL STRUCTURE OF BCP

All the early risks associated with the Bougainville project, including the risk of the project's not proving economically viable, were borne by CRA and NBHC. These companies jointly expended A$21.4 million on the exploration and evaluation of the deposit and gave certain guarantees which enabled BCP to secure the loan financing.[9] Prior to 1973, CRA–NBHC held 67.6 percent of the shares in BCPL. However,

[9] One of the principal guarantees to the creditors was that the mining facilities of BCP would, in fact, become operational.

under a new corporate structure adopted in August 1973, equity capital totals A$133.7 million, of which A$26.7 million, or 20 percent, is held by the PNG government and the Government Investment Corporation; A$71.7 million, or 53.6 percent, by CRA; A$1.7 million, or 1.3 percent, by the PNG public; and A$33.6 million, or 25.1 percent, by general (nonresident) public stockholders. (Different classes of stockholders paid different prices for the stock issue of 267.4 million shares with a par value of 50 A cents each. With the change in the corporate structure the name of the operating company was changed from Bougainville Copper Pty. Ltd. to Bougainville Copper Ltd. (BCL). BCL is incorporated in PNG.

A substantial proportion of the funds for the development of the mine has come from international loans and supplier credits. About U.S.$177 million was provided by a banking consortium headed by the Bank of America, and there is a U.S.$30 million cash loan from Japan. In addition, the Export–Import Bank provided loans totaling U.S.$61 million for purchases of equipment in the United States, and there is a U.S.$23 million Japanese equipment loan. Other loan agreements and guarantees totaled about U.S.$51 million, making an aggregate of U.S.$343 million in loan funds utilized as of August 1973.[10] At the end of 1972 the fixed assets of the company were valued at A$379 million.

Cash outlay by the project initiators, CRA–NBHC, during the exploration and evaluation period was A$21.4 million, and their net cash outlay during the construction period was A$52 million. The PNG government paid A$26.5 million for the purchase of its 20 percent interest in the company at par. Cash outlays by other private equity investors, mostly during the construction period, totaled A$34 million. Shares held by the general public (excluding a special share issue to bona fide residents of PNG) are held by the former shareholders of NBHC (which was liquidated), plus shares equal to 12.4 percent of the equity in BCPL, (which were offered to the public shareholders of CRA and NBHC), plus shares offered to the bank creditors and to the employees and directors and the employee insurance funds or companies associated with the CRA–NBHC group.

Except for the original shareholders of NBHC, the public shareholders purchased their shares at a premium so that the amounts invested by CRA and by the public are not proportional to the respective percentages of the shares held. Thus, while CRA holds par value equity of A$71.7 million in BCL (53.6 percent of A$133.7

[10] As of August 1973, the total loans utilized were A$242 million (A$1 = U.S.$1.42).

million), CRA's net contribution is A$56 million by virtue of its reimbursement for the sale of shares at a premium. As of August 1973 the loan–equity ratio of BCL was 1.8.

THE BEGINNING OF COMMERCIAL OPERATIONS

Commercial production at the Bougainville mine began in April 1972, several months ahead of schedule. During 1972 ore concentrates with a copper metal content of 124,000 metric tons were produced, and production of 183,000 metric tons was achieved in 1973.[11] In 1972 the value of the mine products was A$96 million (net of smelting and refining expenses), with the value of the gold output constituting about one-fifth of the total. During 1973 BCL sold concentrates containing 179,541 metric tons of copper, 19,737 kg of gold, and 43,258 kg of silver for a total value of A$249 million, of which gold represented about 19 percent. At the end of 1973 the mine employed a work force of about 3,800 employees, 76 percent of whom were Papua New Guineans.

The company has contracted for the delivery of concentrates to firms in Japan, West Germany, and Spain over the first fifteen years; deliveries under these contracts account for the vast bulk of expected production. Under the contracts, the price of copper is based on the LME price over an agreed time after delivery, with a minimum price of 30 U.S. cents per pound.

The company has been profitable from the beginning, with earnings of nearly A$28 million in 1972 (after nine months' operation) and earnings of A$158 million in 1973. The company paid a total of A$11 million in dividends to its shareholders with respect to its 1972 operations, and A$80.2 million in dividends went to shareholders for 1973 operations. Much of the remainder of the earnings went for loan repayments and additions to cash reserves. The cash loans have a maturity of seven years or less, so that loan repayments will continue to be sizable until 1979. Loan repayments in 1973 totaled A$68 million. The company must make substantial capital outlays through the 1970s. The declining grade of the ore (from an estimated 0.78 percent of copper in 1972 to 0.50 percent of copper in 1981) will require larger investments in both mining and concentrator equipment in order to provide for the larger volume of ore needed to produce the same or lower copper metal content.

[11] All tons referred to in the Bougainville case study are metric tons.

During 1972 operating costs (excluding depreciation and amortization, interest, and royalties) were about 13.4 A cents (17.1 U.S. cents) per pound of refined copper, including the costs associated with the production of gold and silver. In 1973 operating costs rose to 14.4 A cents (21.8 U.S. cents). The rise in the price in terms of U.S. currency reflected both the appreciation of the Australian dollar in terms of the U.S. dollar and the rise in PNG wages and the prices of materials.[12] Nevertheless, BCL is not a high-cost mine by U.S. standards.

[12] The Australian dollar was appreciated in stages beginning in December 1972, from A$1 = U.S.$1.19 in November 1972 to A$1 = U.S.$1.49 in September 1973.

7
Factors in the Investment Decision for the Bougainville Mine

THE PROJECT EVALUATION

The analysis of the Bougainville ore body and the evaluation and planning of the proposed copper project was unique in its comprehensiveness and in the application of innovative and sophisticated technology. The results from the exploratory diamond drillings were used to divide the ore body into grade zones, with each zone described by the frequency distribution of grade values. A model of the grades of the ore body and their spatial distribution was prepared with the aid of a computer. This model was used to determine the physical limits to mining, taking into account the distribution of mineral values and the characteristics of the rock mass, and to simulate the variations in those factors which could be controlled, such as pit output, concentrate throughput, and cutoff grade, in order to evaluate alternative operating strategies. In this way the company was able to determine the financial outcome of alternative scales of operation, cutoff grade policies, and modes of developing the ore body. The model of the ore body also enabled the company to determine whether higher-grade zones should be mined first, leaving the lower grades for later years, or whether some other strategy would maximize present value of revenue over cost.

Note: The discussion in this section was derived mainly from the article by M. R. L. Blackwell, "Some Aspects of the Evaluation and Planning of the Bougainville Copper Project," in *Decision Making in the Mineral Industry,* special vol. 12 (Montreal: The Canadian Institute of Mining and Metallurgy, 1971), p. 507.

The economic evaluation process involved (1) determining the final pit limits on the basis of drilling results and current cost estimates; and (2) evaluating alternative operating strategies within the pit limits which provided the highest economic returns subject to various constraints. In the evaluation of alternative operating strategies it was necessary to take account of certain constraints or factors not susceptible to control by the management. These included future product prices, the market demand for the products,[1] the amount of equity and loan financing available, and the cost of inputs. Given these "external" factors, the profitability of the project would be determined by management policy with respect to (1) the sequence in which the ore body (containing varying grades of ore) was mined; (2) the physical capacity of various stages in the production process, that is, pit, crushers, concentrator, etc.; and (3) the cutoff grade employed, that is, the lowest grade of ore mined for each mining sequence.

Following a determination of the inventory of the ore reserves, alternative mining strategies were determined in terms of the time sequence, according to which ores of differing grades would be mined for various pit and concentrator capacities. The relative profitability of each strategy was the present value of each of the several sequences expressed as a percentage of a base sequence and determined for different rates of production. This information, which was obtained by simulation analysis, provided the basis for determining the optimum scale of operations within the financial and market constraints. Initial exploitation of the higher-grade portions of the ore body tended to produce higher present values, but with a decline in copper output over time. On the other hand, much higher present values could be achieved by a larger scale of operations which permitted lower cutoff grades and a longer life of the mine. Also, the necessity of maintaining output in order to meet long-term marketing contracts limited the degree to which initial production could be concentrated on high-grade ores. However, with a large-scale operation, copper production could be maintained with the declining grade of ore by increasing the capacity of the mill, for example, adding crushers, ball mills, etc., and the equipment for raising the tonnage of mined ore could be financed over time out of revenues.

The initial investment planned for the Bougainville project called for an expenditure of about A$100 million and a pit output of 30,000

[1] Since a decision was made to produce concentrates rather than blister or refined products, the market demand was determined by the ability of the company to negotiate long-term contracts for concentrates. Had a decision been made to produce refined metal, the size of the market might not have been regarded as a constraint.

tons per day. This was the maximum daily ore throughput for a twenty-five-year mine with proved reserves of 250 million tons. However, a mine evaluation in mid-1967 showed the economic viability of a mine of this capacity to be doubtful. At a later stage when proved reserves were increased to 900 million tons, an evaluation showed that a viable operation could be achieved with a throughput of 80,000 tons per day. The evaluation also showed that net present value rose rapidly with an increase in the scale of operations and with a lower cutoff grade. In fact, net present value for a pit output of 90,000 tons per day was 250 percent of that for a 30,000 ton-per-day operation.[2] Moreover, an even larger scale of operation would have improved the net present value. On the other hand, the availability of financing and of markets constituted a constraint on the scale of operations.

Sometime after the actual negotiation of the agreement with the administration, the project initiator, CRA–NBHC, decided to construct a mine capable of producing and processing 90,000 tons of ore per day and requiring a total investment of A$350 million or more. The carrying out of this decision was contingent upon negotiating long-term contracts for concentrates aggregating some 160,000 metric tons of copper per year and of obtaining cash loan and equipment credits of about A$250 million.

In addition to the mine evaluation, the principal economic factors in the investment decision by the project initiators of the Bougainville mine were the estimated range of future copper prices, tax provisions in the mine contract agreement with the administration, the ability to negotiate long-term contracts for the sale of concentrates, and the availability and terms of the required external financing. During the period of exploration and evaluation from early 1964 to mid-1969 when the final decision was made, the London Metal Exchange (LME) copper price fluctuated from a low of 30 U.S. cents per pound to a high of 70 U.S. cents per pound. During 1968–69 engineering and economic analysis of the project was continued, and contracts were negotiated for the sale of concentrates and for the various sources of debt financing. Not until mid-1969 could all of the variables necessary for the final investment decision be determined with a reasonable degree of confidence. By this time CRA–NBHC had invested over A$20 million in the exploration and evaluation, nearly half of the total equity investment originally contemplated by the project initiators when the total capital outlay for the mine was estimated to be about A$100 million.

---

[2] In calculating net present values (before taxes), discount rates of 15–17 percent were employed.

ESTIMATING PROFITABILITY OF
THE BOUGAINVILLE PROJECT

In the final evaluation report prior to the decision to undertake the investment in the Bougainville mine, detailed cash flow statements were prepared at various copper prices and discounted cash flow (DCF) calculations for a twenty-year life were made for each price assumption. The project was examined for sensitivity in relation to the following variables: ore grade, capital costs, operating costs, metal recovery, concentrator capacity, product prices, and concentrate grade. Prices of 30 U.S. cents, 38 U.S. cents, and 45 U.S. cents per pound were used for copper and U.S.$38 per ounce for gold. Copper prices were escalated at 2 percent per annum. The upper range of copper prices employed in the analysis appears unduly conservative in view of the fact that the LME price for wirebars was in excess of 70 U.S. cents per pound in the second half of 1969. Certainly, it must not have seemed too optimistic that an average price of 55 U.S. cents per pound would have prevailed during the early years of operation. Indeed, in the Australian government's white paper on the Bougainville copper project, presented in March 1970 to the PNG House of Assembly, prices of 55 and 30 U.S. cents per pound were used as the basis for projecting PNG government revenue from the mine.[3] According to an internal CRA document, the DCF rate of return for an operating life of twenty years on "total capital at risk, including working capital,"[4] varied between 5 and 20 percent, depending upon the price and variations in the parameters. Presumably, DCF rates of return were calculated for the equity investment of CRA–NBHC, but I have no evidence of this. At the time the Bougainville decision was made, CRA reportedly judged projects on the basis of the internal rate of return on total funds at risk, and 10 percent was regarded as an acceptable DCF rate for mining investment in Australia under normal circumstances. However, since the Bougainville project carried a political risk in excess of that for investments in Australia, a higher DCF was regarded as necessary to warrant the investment in Bougainville. Evidence suggests that CRA regarded a 15 percent rate of return as

---

[3] "Bougainville Copper Project," a statement delivered by the assistant administrator (economic affairs) of the Department of External Territories, in the PNG House of Assembly, March 5, 1970, p. 7.

[4] This presumably would include borrowed capital as well as equity. However, CRA's obligation to the creditors was limited to the construction of the mine and bringing it into operation. CRA did not guarantee BCL's indebtedness. In considering expected rates of return, it should be noted that they are related to rates of interest in the international money markets. In the late 1960s interest rates were generally much lower than those of the early 1970s.

the minimum expectation necessary to warrant an investment in Bougainville, again presumably on total capital at risk.

I do not have complete information on the process by which the policy makers in CRA arrived at the final decision to go ahead with the investment in the Bougainville project. Engineers, accountants, and economists may compile volumes of technical analysis, but policy makers do not depend upon mathematical models alone in reaching their decisions. Given the uncertainties underlying the assumptions in the technical analysis, policy makers tend to rely heavily on their own experience, intuition, and on objectives such as personal pride in successfully carrying out a program with which they have been associated, or even on a desire to promote public welfare—objectives not found in the programming models of the professional analyst. Therefore, we cannot be sure of the relative weights given to the various factors relevant to the investment decision by the policy makers. We can only reconstruct on the basis of inadequate knowledge what appears to be a reasonable assessment of profit expectations for a range of future price assumptions at the time the decision was made.

In this assessment I shall rely heavily on a paper prepared by Dr. B. R. Stewardson of the Department of Economics, LaTrobe University, and delivered to the Forty-Second Congress of the Australian and New Zealand Association for the Advancement of Science held in Port Moresby in August 1970.[5] Stewardson derived his estimates of costs and revenues for the Bougainville mine from Australian government documents, from published statements by the company, and from his own intimate knowledge of the copper industry. On the basis of his estimates of production costs, debt service payments on A$250 million in loans and suppliers' credits, and projected revenues from product sales, Stewardson calculated returns to an estimated A$84 million in equity investment by CRA–NBHC for four possible prices of copper, ranging from 30–65 U.S. cents per pound.

Given the tax provisions stipulated in the mining agreement with the administration, and assuming no difficulties were incurred in mine construction—for example, cost overruns, floods, or in the metallurgical system—the principal economic factor determining the expected profitability of the mine was the projected price of the product. Operating costs would vary with changes in wage rates and materials prices, but the effects of a 10 percent rise in wage rates would normally be no more than one-fifth of the impact on cash flow which would

---

[5] The title of Stewardson's paper is "The Bougainville Copper Agreement." A slightly revised version of the paper (to take care of errors made in the original presentation) was kindly made available to me by Stewardson.

Table 10. Projected Financial Returns to CRA–NBHC Equity Investment
for Alternative Prices of Copper
(millions of Australian dollars)

		Copper prices	
Period	*30 U.S. cents*	*40 U.S. cents*	*55 U.S. cents*
Pretax period[a]			
Annual return, A$	0	14	46
Accounting rate of return, %[b]	0	16	55
Full-tax period			
Annual return, A$	24	36	56
Accounting rate of return, %[b]	29	43	67
Internal rate of return over			
twenty-year production period, %	7.7	15.2	27.2

Source: B. R. Stewardson, "The Bougainville Copper Agreement."
Note: Financial results that might have been reasonably projected in mid-1969,
at the time the final decision to construct the Bougainville mine was made.
[a] Eight years.
[b] A$84 million investment.

result from a 10 percent fall in product prices. From the viewpoint of a
mining firm in mid-1969, a 30 U.S. cents-per-pound price for copper
would have been regarded as the lower limit for any substantial period
in the future. Also, the long-term contracts for the sale of concentrates
contained a floor price of 30 U.S. cents. With the LME price in
mid-1969 well above 60 U.S. cents per pound and the low for 1969
above 55 U.S. cents per pound, a 55 U.S. cents-per-pound copper price
appeared to be a moderately optimistic forecast, and the most probable future price range was in the neighborhood of 40–55 U.S. cents
per pound. Moreover, the Bougainville mine was expected to be a
relatively low-cost producer with direct operating costs under 12 U.S.
cents per pound, well below the world average.

Table 10 shows Stewardson's estimates of the annual returns to
CRA–NBHC (based on an equity investment of A$84 million) for the
pretax period and for the full-tax period for alternative prices of
copper. Assuming that the pretax period is eight years—during which
time all indebtedness is paid off—I have calculated the internal rate
of return to CRA–NBHC over a twenty-year operating period for three
alternative prices of copper. For 30 U.S. cents per pound, no dividends
could be paid to CRA–NBHC for the first eight years of operation.
Cash outflow during the four-year exploration and evaluation period
is assumed to be A$5 million per year, followed by a four-year con-
struction period, during which time cash outflow by CRA–NBHC is
A$16 million per year. This yielded an internal rate of return of 7.7
percent for 30 U.S. cents-per-pound copper over a twenty-year pro-

duction period. Such a rate of return would ordinarily not be attractive to investors, but cash flow would at least be large enough to liquidate the indebtedness and to provide a modest profit beginning with the ninth year of operation. For 40 U.S. cents-per-pound copper, the internal rate of return rises to 15.2 percent, corresponding to the minimum rate of return CRA reportedly required as a condition for making an equity investment in PNG. For the higher limit of the probable price range, 55 U.S. cents per pound, the internal rate of return rises to 27.2 percent. It should be noted that Stewardson's estimates did not take into account the 15 percent PNG dividend withholding tax, which at the time did not apply to dividends paid by BCPL (a PNG corporation) to Bougainville Mining Ltd. (an Australian corporation). The 15 percent withholding tax would have reduced the internal rate of return to 12.9 percent, based on 40 U.S. cents-per-pound copper, and to 23.1 percent for 55 U.S. cents-per-pound copper.

Although there is a large amount of conjecture in the above estimates, they are probably not too far from the prospective conditions on which the investment decision was made in mid-1969. In 1967 when the agreement with the Australian government was negotiated, the LME price and the price outlook were much less favorable, and a future copper price range of 30–40 U.S. cents per pound may have appeared realistic. Without the tax holiday plus accelerated depreciation, cash flow at 30 U.S. cents per pound would not have been sufficient to meet the debt service. At 40 U.S. cents per pound the debt service could have been met, but without the tax holiday and accelerated depreciation the internal return to equity over the twenty-year operating period would probably not have been attractive, since dividends would have been substantially lower during the first eight years of operations.[6]

NONECONOMIC FACTORS IN THE INVESTMENT DECISION

There can be little doubt that CRA officials were anxious to find and develop new ore bodies in Australia and its Territories as a means of promoting the growth of the company. It is also true that the Australian government was very anxious to promote the development of PNG, which in the next decade or so it expected to become politically

[6] Stewardson's estimates of returns to original equity holders are probably overstated, since not only did he disregard the 15 percent withholding tax, but he also did not account for additional capital outlays after the initiation of operations.

independent of Australia and economically self-supporting. It was particularly important that PNG acquire sources of foreign exchange income, for without such income it would continue to be dependent upon large subsidies from the Australian government. In the course of conversations with such CRA officials as Sir Maurice Mawby, Frank Espie, Ray Ballmer, and Donald Vernon, who have been concerned both with the welfare of the people of PNG and with the problems of exploring and evaluating the mine and of mobilizing financial and technical resources for its construction, I sensed a strong personal desire on the part of these officials to see the project succeed in the interest of the welfare of Australia, the people of PNG, and of the company. These forces and motivations go beyond profit and loss calculations, although quite obviously companies cannot risk hundreds of millions of dollars of their own capital and that of others unless there is a good chance for financial success.

Despite the fact that PNG was a dependency of Australia, CRA officials were deeply concerned regarding potential political risks of the investment. There was a wave of expropriations of mining properties throughout the developing world in the late 1960s, including the partial nationalization of the Zambian copper industry, the demand by the Frei government of Chile for 51 percent of Anaconda's Chuquicamata mine, the expropriation of the International Petroleum Company in Peru, and the nationalization of Union Miniere's mining properties in Zaire (formerly the Republic of the Congo). As has already been noted, the Australian government did not provide the company with an investment guarantee against expropriation and government violation of the mining contract in the agreement.

Many local PNG politicians were consulted on the agreement, and it was subject to ratification by the PNG House of Assembly. Even the most prominent legislative representative from Bougainville, Paul Lapun (who later became PNG minister of mines), voted in favor of the agreement. Nevertheless, there was substantial opposition both to the agreement and to the construction of the Bougainville mine on any terms. Moreover, there is a strong secessionist movement in Bougainville by people who believe they should not be a part of PNG. Had CRA officials known that PNG would have become independent in a little more than four years following the final decision to make the investment, it is quite likely that the Bougainville mine would not have been constructed in the absence of an investment guarantee by the Australian government.

8
The Economic Contribution of the Bougainville Mine to PNG

Since Bougainville Copper Ltd. (BCL) only began operations in April 1972, and its full revenue potential for the Papua New Guinea (PNG) government will not be realized until the late 1970s, the analysis of the full impact of BCL on the PNG economy must be based in part on a simulation of BCL's financial operations in future years. In this chapter I shall be concerned with (1) the economic impact of BCL during the construction period; (2) the amount and distribution of "retained value"; (3) BCL's contribution to PNG's balance of payments and national income; (4) the fiscal impact on the PNG government; (5) the impact on employment and training; and (6) the contribution of BCL to domestic production.[1]

THE ECONOMIC IMPACT
DURING THE CONSTRUCTION PERIOD

Impact on Employment

The mine construction period from early 1969 to the beginning of mine operations in April 1972 is a unique and nonrecurring phase in the history of the mine. The economic and social impact on Bougainville was enormous, but the direct effects on PNG as a whole were

[1] Many of the data employed in this chapter are taken from, or based on, a paper entitled "A Study of the Impact of the Bougainville Copper Project on the Economy and Society of Papua New Guinea," W. D. Scott and Company Pty. Ltd. (January 1973). It will be referred to as the Scott report.

minor. Since we are mainly concerned in this study with the longer-run consequences of BCL for PNG, I shall not deal with this period in great detail. The major immediate impacts were the sharp rise in employment, with the bulk of the indigenous workers coming from outside Bougainville; the large increase in wage payments and expenditures for local materials and services; the leasing of land by the mine; the damage to the agricultural economy in the area occupied by the mine; and the large PNG government expenditures on infrastructure related to the new mining communities and to the requirements of the mine.

Employment of indigenes for construction by BCL and the construction organization, Bechtel–WKE,[2] and its contractors was 31,000 man-months during the year ended June 1970; 62,800 man-months during the year ended June 1971; and 50,700 man-months during the year ended June 1972. At the peak of employment, in July 1971, about 6,400 indigenes and 4,100 nonindigenes were employed in construction. The indigenous workers during the construction period came from districts throughout PNG; only 27 percent came originally from Bougainville. In June 1970 the total PNG indigenous work force employed in the mining and building construction industries was 15,780; in this same year the indigenous work force of BCL was about 2,600, accounting for nearly 17 percent of the PNG work force in these industries. However, at the peak of the construction period the BCL project's contribution to mining and building employment rose to about 30 percent.[3] The total work force of 10,500 workers during the peak of the BCL construction period may be contrasted with employment in the mine at the end of 1972 when it reached about 3,500.

The demand for labor during the construction phase was supplied from (1) wage and salary earners leaving previous employment; (2) unemployed urban dwellers; and (3) rural dwellers. Although no data are available, knowledgeable people both within and outside the company have expressed the view that the last two sources were far more numerous than the first.[4] An effort was made not to pay wages for particular skills that were out of line with the general level of wages in PNG for indigenes in those skill categories. Nevertheless, in June 1970 the average PNG indigenous wage level in mining and

[2] Consortium of Bechtel Corporation and Western Knapp Engineering.
[3] Data for PNG indigenous work force for June 1970 were obtained from Government of Papua New Guinea, Department of Labor, *Labor Information Bulletin,* no. 7 (1971).
[4] An official of the PNG Manpower Planning Unit told me that probably no more than 200 PNG indigenous workers left skilled or semiskilled jobs to take positions with BCL during the construction period.

quarrying was less than A$30 per month while BCL figures show that the average indigenous employee on its payroll in 1970 received over four times this amount. While it has been claimed that the BCL project exerted an upward pressure on indigenous wage rates throughout PNG, the higher wages paid to indigenes probably reflected the tendency for the gap between indigenous and nonindigenous wage rates to narrow.

Since the bulk of the workers was untrained, both BCL and Bechtel–WKE had to undertake an extensive training program (see p. 116). However, since the majority of those hired during the construction period returned to their homes throughout PNG at the end of the construction phase, it seems likely that the withdrawal of skilled and experienced workers from other sectors of the economy was more than compensated for by the training and experience of the workers returned to the economy.

Gross fixed capital expenditure during the construction period (1969–70/1971–72) totaled A$356 million. Of this amount, about A$80 million went for salaries and wages (A$19 million to indigenes and A$61 million to nonindigenous employees); A$30 million was spent for local purchases of which the import content was A$14 million; A$174 million went for imports of goods and services; and the remainder— A$73 million—was accounted for by interest payments on loans, depreciation, contractors' profits, etc.[5] To these expenditures must be added an estimated A$27 million in outlays by the PNG government for the town of Arawa to build roads, telecommunications, water supply and power facilities, etc. over the same period. Altogether, local expenditures on the small agricultural community of South Bougainville were well in excess of A$100 million and had an enormous economic and social impact. For obvious reasons, the response of local production to this increase in monetary demand was small, since, with few exceptions, the facilities for increasing output to meet the commodities demanded did not exist.

Agricultural Impact

The creation of the Bougainville mine has resulted in both favorable and unfavorable impacts on agriculture in South Bougainville. The take-over by the PNG government of the area occupied by the Arawa plantation, with sales of cacao and copra estimated at A$500,000 annually, and of certain other agricultural lands resulted in a sig-

---

[5] The above estimates include some outlays during the initial period of operations, April–June 1972. Data from the Scott report, appendix 5A.

DIRECT EFFECTS   INDIRECT EFFECTS

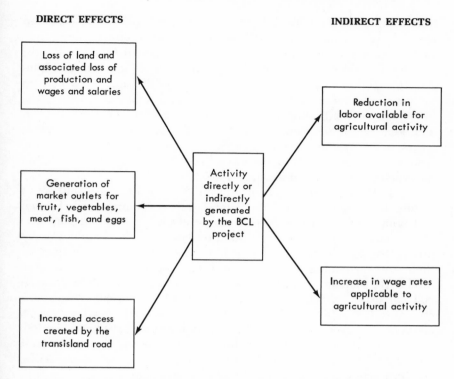

Figure 1. Effect of BCL activity on the agricultural sphere in Papua New Guinea (*Source of data:* the Scott report.)

nificant loss of cash crop production. Partly offsetting this impact was the purchase of fruits and vegetables by BCL from local producers, amounting to A$230,000 in 1970 and A$336,000 in 1971. In the long run, the increased demand for fruits and vegetables generated by mining communities could provide a market of an estimated A$700,000 a year (in current prices) for local growers. In addition, there is a large demand for meat, fish, and poultry that could be supplied from local sources, when and if production facilities are established.

The region's major crops, cacao and copra, have gained from increased access to markets and ports provided by the transisland road built by BCL and by the creation or upgrading of other roads in South Bougainville. On the other hand, the mine has withdrawn labor previously available for agriculture and has contributed to an increase in wage rates applicable to agriculture.

Any immediate loss in agricultural output to farmers has been more than compensated for by cash payments from BCL for land occupied under lease; for destruction and damage to cash crops, gardens, livestock, etc.; for destruction or detrimental effects to fishing grounds; and for the relocation of villages. During the exploration and construction period to February 1972, over A$900,000 had been paid to indigenes for these and other purposes, and substantial additional lump sum payments of A$200–A$300,000 are to be paid in the future. In addition, landowners whose lands are covered by company mining leases are currently receiving A$223,000 per year; owners of the land are also entitled to 5 percent of the royalties paid to the PNG government, estimated at about A$100,000 annually.

Article 15 of the BCP agreement of 1967 obligates the company to restore to agricultural use the land used for dumping overburden and tailings after such land is no longer needed for mining purposes. The company is therefore attempting to make such land agriculturally productive and is also assisting landowners who have leased part of their land for mining purposes to use their remaining land in a more productive manner. For these reasons, the company employs an agricultural extension team and has established an agricultural experimental station at Kobuan, near Kieta. Cattle, pig, and poultry projects are underway, and experimental fruit and nut trees have been planted. More particularly, local farmers have been encouraged to grow fruit and vegetables for local consumption by the mine's work force. Seeds, fertilizer, and insecticide are distributed at cost price.

THE AMOUNT AND DISTRIBUTION OF RETAINED VALUE

In this section I shall analyze *retained value* (or that portion of export revenue accruing to the PNG economy) in much the same manner that retained value was analyzed for the Toquepala mine. Because of the tax holiday followed by accelerated depreciation, the ratio of retained value to total BCL revenue is substantially lower during the first eight years or so of operations (April 1972–June 1980) than it is thereafter. I shall therefore estimate retained value first on the basis of current operations and then for a representative year following the tax holiday and period of accelerated depreciation. Since company data on financial operations of BCL are available for the period April 1972–December 31, 1973, I shall begin by estimating retained value for this period in relation to total revenue and to the allocation of external transfers of revenue.

RETAINED VALUE FOR
APRIL 1972–DECEMBER 1973

We may define retained value, RV, as follows:

$$RV = W - SE + DP - M_d + RO + L + DD + CT + WT + CU$$

where

W = total wages, salaries, and salary supplements
SE = salaries of expatriates accruing abroad
DP = domestic purchases of goods and services
M_d = import content of DP
RO = royalty payments to PNG
L = payments to landowners
DD = dividends paid to PNG government and to PNG resident equity holders
CT = corporate income tax
WT = withholding tax on dividends to nonresidents
CU = customs duty.

Total BCL revenue, R, is equal to retained value plus all payments abroad. We may express this relationship symbolically as follows:

$$R = RV + M + M_d + I_n + FD + LR + SE + U$$

where

R = exports f.o.b. (excluding realization expenses)
M = imports (excluding import content of local purchases)
I_n = interest paid on loans and credits less interest received on cash reserves
FD = dividends paid to nonresidents less withholding tax
LR = loan repayments
U = additions to cash reserves less exchange gains on loans and interest plus unidentified items[6]

As shown in Table 11, retained value for the April 1972–December 1973 period totaled A\$82 million, of which A\$38 million were wage payments less expatriates' salaries accruing abroad, A\$4 million were domestic purchases less import content, A\$1 million was paid to PNG resident shareholders, A\$2 million was paid to landholders, A\$34 million went to the government, and A\$3 million was donated to the PNG Development Foundation.[7]

[6] Exchange gains on loans are not included in R but were employed in 1973 for making prepayments on loan obligations.
[7] Amounts have been rounded to the nearest million because certain of the amounts are rough estimates.

Table 11. Distribution of BCL's Total Revenue (R) and Retained Value
(RV) Components During April 1, 1972–December 31, 1973

Distribution of RV Component		Distribution of R[a]	
Component	Revenue	Component	Revenue
$W - SE$	38	RV	82
$DP - M_d$	4	M	37
RO	4	M_d	3
L	2		
DD	19[b]	I_n	31
WT	11	SE	5
CT	0	FD	61[c]
CU	1	LR	70
G	3	U	56
Total	$A82 million	Total	A$345 million

Sources: BCL annual reports; the Scott report; and other BCL sources.

Note: For abbreviations used in table, see page 105.

[a] R does not include exchange gains on the foreign loans and interest income, most of which is reflected in the accumulation of reserves. Exchange gains on loans were A$14 million for the entire period, and interest income was A$3 million.

[b] Includes final dividends declared on 1973 earnings and payable April 1974. Nongovernment dividend receipts of PNG residents were A$900,000.

[c] Includes dividend payable in April 1974 on 1973 earnings.

It will be noted also from Table 11 that, of the A$345 million in BCL revenue over the period April 1972–December 1973, A$82 million, or 24 percent, represented retained value. About A$61 million, or 18 percent, was paid in dividends to nonresident stockholders. The remaining A$202 million, or 58 percent, was employed for imports, debt service, and other operating foreign payments, plus additions to cash reserves required by the credit agreement. BCL continued to make new capital expenditures during 1972–73, financed mainly by drawing on unspent balances of the loans negotiated for the construction of the mine.[8] Capital expenditures will continue to be made for new equipment, such as additional ball mills required to process the ore as the grade declines, and to replace old equipment. In the future, however, such expenditures must be financed out of depreciation allowances and reinvested earnings.

BCL cash reserves, which totaled about A$65 million at the end of 1973, are largely held by the Bank of Papua New Guinea, and BCL's foreign exchange operations are conducted under the requirements of PNG foreign exchange regulations which became effective November

[8] The distribution of capital expenditures and of the exchange gains on the loans and interest income are not included in Tables 8 and 9, since these tables are concerned only with the distribution of BCL revenue from the sale of concentrates.

1, 1973. Since the bulk of the additions to cash reserves over the 1972–73 period are held in a PNG bank, this accumulation is in a sense returned to the PNG economy. However, for purposes of this analysis I have not included the additions to cash reserves as a part of retained value.

Retained Value for a Representative Year (1983)

The distribution of total revenues for the 1972–73 period, shown in Tables 8 and 9, must inevitably change rather drastically in the future when the debt has been retired, and BCL becomes subject to the corporate taxes provided in the new 1974 agreement. In addition, it is anticipated that with the development of the PNG economy the ratio of domestic purchases to imports will rise, as will the ratio of aggregate earnings of PNG employees to the earnings of expatriates. In order to analyze the changes in the distribution of total revenue, I have prepared a simulation of BCL's operations for a representative year (say, 1983), by which time I have assumed that all debts will have been retired. Since I want to avoid projecting either product prices or costs, I have simply assumed the same level of revenue and operating costs as in 1973. Although this assumption may be regarded as unrealistic, my purpose is to examine the change in the distribution of revenue, not in the absolute shares.[9] I have, therefore, assumed that in 1983 revenues will be A$250 million and direct operating costs A$60 million, approximately the same as in 1973. However, I have assumed certain changes within the pattern of operating expenditures in accordance with coefficients derived from the Scott report. Finally, I have assumed that all net earnings after taxes are distributed to stockholders and that capital expenditures are equal to the depreciation allowance, estimated to be A$25 million for 1983.

Table 12 reflects a simulation of revenues, expenditures, earnings, and dividends for a representative year (1983) under the assumptions given above. These simulated results show earnings before company tax of A$162 million, an amount which corresponds closely with actual net earnings in 1973 (A$158.4 million). However, the company tax of A$82 million, shown in Table 12, reduces net earnings after taxes to A$80 million, all of which is assumed to be paid out in dividends.

---

[9] Production is expected to decline somewhat with the decrease in the grade of the ore, and the wages and prices of material inputs are rising rapidly. Also, many mining officials believe that the *relative* price of copper will decline from 1973 levels. On the other hand, the relative price of gold in future years is likely to be substantially higher than in 1973.

Table 12. Simulated Revenues, Expenditures, and Distribution of Earnings of BCL for a Representative Year (1983)[a] (millions of Australian dollars)

Revenue (total costs plus earnings)			250
Direct operating costs		60	
Depreciation		25	
Royalties		3	
Total costs			88
Earnings before company tax			162
Company tax[b]		82	
Net earnings after taxes		80	
Dividends:		80	
Government	16		
Withholding tax	9		
PNG resident dividends	1		
External dividend payments	54		

[a] See text for assumptions.
[b] Based on the formula in the 1974 agreement.

Table 13 shows a simulated distribution of BCL expenditures and earnings (shown in Table 10) for the representative year (1983). According to the simulation results given in Table 13, it may be noted that retained value is 62 percent of BCL revenues, as contrasted with 26 percent for the period April 1972–December 1973 (shown in Table 11). The PNG government revenues rise from 11 percent of total BCL revenue in the April 1972–December 1973 period to 45 percent for the representative year. Dividend payments to foreign equity holders rise from 18 percent of total revenue in the period April 1972–December 1973 to 22 percent for the simulated representative year. Earnings available for dividends are increased by the elimination of debt service payments on the one hand, but are reduced by the corporate tax obligation on the other.

Retained Value During the Construction Period

During the construction period (January 1969–March 1972) retained value was generated from capital expenditures of A$356 million, financed by capital inflow, plus about A$26 million in equity financing from the PNG government. As defined above, retained value during the three-year period totaled A$124 million.[10] Looked at another way,

[10] Retained value was accounted for as follows: wages, salaries, and supplements of A$87 million; less A$13 million in expatriate income accruing abroad; plus A$38 million in domestic purchases; less A$17 million import content of domestic purchases; plus A$28 million in taxes, plus A$1 million in rent payments. There were no dividends paid to domestic residents during this period. (Data taken from Scott report.)

Table 13. Simulated Distribution of BCL Revenues for a Representative Year
(1983): Retained Value and External Payments
(millions of Australian dollars)

Distribution		Revenues
Total retained value		**154**
Wages and salaries plus supplements less salaries		
of expatriates accruing abroad		24
Domestic purchases less import content		16
Land rents		1
PNG resident dividends		1
Government revenues:		112
Corporate tax	82	
Dividends	16	
Withholding tax	9	
Royalties	3	
Customs duties	2	
Total external payments		**96**
Imports (including import content of		
domestic purchases)		40
Salaries of expatriates accruing abroad		2
Dividends		54
Total revenue		**250**

Sources: Basic operating data derived from Table 12. Simulations of wages and
salaries, domestic purchases and land rents determined by use of coefficients derived from Scott report.

we might regard virtually the entire A$356 million in capital expendi-
tures during the construction period as retained value, since what PNG
acquired was a valuable mine capable of producing revenue for the
economy for many decades to come. Although the foreign suppliers
of the capital hold claims on a part of the future revenues from the
mine, the mine is fundamentally a part of the resources of PNG.
However, in terms of current monetary impact, the retained value
during the construction period was only A$124 million. Most of the
remainder of the A$356 million in capital expenditures was used to
finance imports of goods and services required for the construction of
the mine.

BCL'S CONTRIBUTION TO
THE BALANCE OF PAYMENTS
AND NATIONAL PRODUCT

The direct contribution of BCL to both the balance of payments and
the national income of PNG are roughly equal to the retained value;
that is, BCL gross revenue plus net capital imports minus imported

inputs and external payments to foreign factors of production. During the period April 1972–December 1973, the average annual direct contribution to national income was about A$47 million. If we exclude the increase in BCL cash reserves held in the Bank of Papua New Guinea, the average annual balance-of-payments contribution was also about A$47 million. However, on the basis of our simulated analysis for a representative year (1983), given in Table 14, the annual direct contribution to the balance of payments and to the national income rises to A$154 million. These direct contributions are substantial in relation to the total export earnings and to the GNP of the PNG economy. In 1970–71 merchandise exports of PNG were A$77 million,[11] and a preliminary estimate of the gross monetary sector product for the same year was A$416 million.[12]

In considering the indirect impact of BCL on PNG's balance of payments, account must be taken of the imports of goods and services induced by the payments to the domestic factors of production and to the government. A recent study shows that the import content of personal consumption in the monetary sector was 54 percent and that of government expenditures 23 percent. However, since a high proportion of government expenditures takes the form of wages and salaries, the indirect impact of government expenditures is substantially higher.[13] Overall, the import content of PNG market expenditures in 1970 was 45 percent. The same study projects a reduction in the import content of personal consumption in PNG from 54 percent in 1970 to 52 percent in 1978, and in the overall import content of market expenditures from 45 percent in 1970 to 35 percent by 1978.[14] The import content of personal consumption of the wage and salary workers at the Bougainville mine is undoubtedly higher than the average for PNG, since most of what is consumed on Bougainville must be imported and a high proportion of the imports come from outside PNG.

The ultimate contribution of the Bougainville mine to both the

[11] K. L. Mahar, "Capital Flows, Resource Flows, and the Monetarisation of Papua New Guinea." Paper presented at the Forty-fifth Congress of the Australian and New Zealand Association for the Advancement of Science, at Perth, Australia, 1973, appendix A.

[12] C. C. Wilson, "Papua New Guinea: Fast Growth Versus Indigenisation: Conflict or Harmony?" Paper presented at the Forty-fifth Congress of the Australian and New Zealand Association for the Advancement of Science, at Perth, Australia, 1973, appendix, table 1.

[13] M. L. Parker, "The Papua New Guinea Economy, 1978." Paper presented at the Forty-fifth Congress of the Australian and New Zealand Association for the Advancement of Science, in Perth, Australia, 1973, table 7, p. 13.

[14] Ibid.

national product and to the PNG balance of payments will depend upon an increase in the domestic value-added content of market expenditures. For there to be a substantial rise in real national income beyond the direct contribution, there must be an increase in investment in agriculture and industry together with an increase in productivity. Increased investment should be induced by the increased demand for local goods and services and the new investment financed by the additional savings generated by the larger incomes and by the availability of foreign exchange for imported equipment, materials, and technology. (The possibilities for increasing domestic production through backward and forward linkages created by the Bougainville mine will be examined on pages 120–121).

It is not possible to reliably project the ultimate impact on real national income by means of simple multiplier analysis. If nothing is done to increase productive capacity and productivity, the vast bulk of the domestic income generated by the mine may simply be used to purchase additional inputs for consumption. On the other hand, if investment and productivity rise as a consequence of the stimulus provided by the increase in domestic purchasing power, the rise in national income could be substantial—perhaps 50–100 percent of BCL's direct contribution to national income. Only if we know how the PNG economy will respond, sector by sector, to the direct increase in income generated by the mine can we estimate the indirect or secondary contribution to national income. Likewise, the Bougainville mine's real contribution to PNG balance of payments will depend upon how much of the foreign exchange income is released for imports of investment goods. The Bougainville mine cannot make a substantial contribution to PNG's balance of payments if the bulk of the foreign exchange receipts are absorbed by imports for personal consumption. Moreover, PNG cannot rely on the Bougainville mine alone to meet her future foreign exchange requirements for continued growth. If a reasonable rate of growth is to be sustained, it will be necessary for PNG to develop other export industries.

THE FISCAL IMPACT ON
THE PNG GOVERNMENT

The fiscal impact of the Bougainville mine on the PNG government is determined by (1) direct revenues in the form of dividends and taxes plus receipts from personal taxes on BCL employees and taxes on BCL purchases; and (2) government outlays for BCL equity shares, capital

Table 14. Direct BCL Contributions to the PNG Government in 1973, and for a Representative Year (1983) (millions of Australian dollars)

Item	1973	(1983)
Royalties	3.1	3.0
Dividends	16.0	16.0
Corporate profits tax	—	82.0
Dividend withholding tax	9.6[a]	9.0
Employee tax[b]	3.1	3.0
Customs duties and other indirect taxes	2.8	3.0
TOTAL	34.6	116.0

Sources: BCL, and Table 13 (p. 109). See text for assumptions relating to representative year (1983).

[a] Includes A$100,000 withholding tax on share issues.

[b] Includes small amount of lease rents.

expenditures related to the mining community, and certain current expenditures related to mine activities. A full analysis of the direct and indirect fiscal impacts would require a projection of the public sector in relation to projected gross monetary product. This in turn would require a number of assumptions regarding the future tax structure of PNG, together with a projection of the increase in public expenditures in South Bougainville that might be related to the growth of population and public services arising from the mine. Since such projections would be subject to a very large degree of error, I shall confine the analysis of fiscal impact to revenues and expenditures directly associated with the activities of the mine.

PNG Revenues from BCL

The principal sources of the PNG government revenue derived directly from BCL are (1) royalties, (2) dividends paid by BCL, (3) taxes on BCL profits, (4) withholding taxes on dividends paid to foreign shareholders, (5) personal taxes on BCL employees, (6) taxes on BCL purchases of goods and services (both imports and local purchases), and (7) lease rents. Table 14 shows direct BCL contributions to PNG government revenues for 1973 and for a representative year (1983). These contributions do not include payments to the government for certain public services, including telephone, power, and certain other taxes and fees, such as automobile registration fees and shipping taxes. Partly offsetting these PNG government revenues are the government's outlays for the purchase of equity in BCL; and capital expenditures for infrastructure related to the mining communities. These will be described later (see pages 115–116).

Analysis of the BCL Tax Regime
Under the 1967 Agreement

The tax rates applying to BCL and its nonresident stockholders under the 1967 agreement are based on a combination of the PNG's general tax structure and the special tax provisions of the agreement itself. The agreement allows for the continuation of the exemption from tax of 20 percent of taxable income derived from copper mining, despite the fact that this provision has recently been repealed from the general tax structure. The 1973 general corporate tax rate was 25 percent of taxable profits, but the 1967 agreement provides for a gradual transition to a 50 percent rate over a period of four years, following a three-year tax holiday during which no company taxes are levied. The first escalation in the tax rate toward 50 percent does not begin until the second year in which a tax is actually paid, that is, after the three-year tax holiday and after the period of accelerated depreciation during which the initial capital expenditures are written off against earnings.[15] Assuming the period of accelerated depreciation (permitted under Division 10 of the Income Tax Ordinance) requires four years, no company tax is payable until the eighth year of production, and the first escalation in the tax rate begins in the ninth year. Beginning with the twenty-sixth year after commercial production was initiated, the 50 percent tax rate will rise by 1 percent per annum to a maximum rate of 66 percent. Payment of dividends to nonresidents of PNG are subject to a withholding tax of 15 percent.

In the first year of taxable income following the three-year tax holiday period and the period of accelerated depreciation, BCL is subject to the normal 25 percent tax, but since 20 percent of taxable income is exempt from taxation, only 80 percent of BCL's taxable income is subject to the 25 percent tax.[16] Hence, the effective company tax rate is 20 percent of taxable income.

In the second year in which a tax is paid, the tax rate rises from 25 percent to 31.25 percent, or by 25 percent of the difference between the normal 25 percent tax rate and a 50 percent tax rate; this results in an effective rate of 25 percent of BCL's taxable income. In the third year, the tax rate rises to 37.5 percent, or to an effective rate of 30 percent. In the fourth year, the tax rate rises to 43.75 percent, or to an effective rate of 35 percent. In the fifth year, the tax rate rises to 50 percent, or to an effective rate of 40 percent, and this rate continues

---

[15] The period of accelerated depreciation begins *after* the three-year tax holiday.

[16] The general PNG company tax may be changed by legislative action, but the 50 percent tax provided for in the 1967 agreement may not be changed without violating the agreement.

Table 15. Operation of the PNG Tax Arrangement for BCL[a]

Division of taxable income	First year	Second year	Third year	Fourth year	Fifth year	Year of maximum tax rate
Taxable profits	100	100	100	100	100	100
Company tax[b]	20	25	30	35	40	52.8
PNG government dividend	16	15	14	13	12	9.4
Foreign shareholders' dividend	64	60	56	52	48	37.8
Withholding tax on foreign dividend	9.6	9.0	8.4	7.8	7.2	5.7
Total amount paid to foreign shareholders	54.4	51.0	47.6	44.2	40.8	32.1
Total amount accruing to PNG government	45.6	49.0	52.4	55.8	59.2	67.9

[a] In this table the *first year* is the initial year in which a tax is payable, that is, the first year following the three-year tax holiday and the period of accelerated depreciation.
[b] Effective tax after exemption of 20 percent of taxable income.

until the twenty-sixth year of production when the tax rate rises by 1 percent in each of the following years until it reaches a maximum of 66 percent, or an effective rate of 52.8 percent.

In order to illustrate the operation of the tax arrangement, let us assume that BCL's taxable income in each of the years following the tax holiday and the period of accelerated depreciation is 100, and that all after-company tax profits are paid out in dividends to the PNG government and to the private stockholders, all of whom are assumed to be foreign residents.[17] Table 15 shows how the company's taxable income of 100 per year is divided in each of the five years in accordance with the formula described above. Thus it will be seen that the government's share of taxable profits rises from 45.6 percent in the first year of taxable income to 59.2 percent in the fifth year, and continues at that rate until the twenty-sixth year of production. Under the assumptions outlined above, in the year of maximum tax rate (66 percent), the government will receive 67.9 percent of taxable profits as against 32.1 percent for the foreign shareholder.

Comparison with the Tax Regime
Under the 1974 Agreement

Under the 1974 agreement the corporate tax on BCL will be the higher of (1) the normal company income tax (33⅓ percent); or (2) the

[17] About 1.3 percent of the shares of BCL are held by PNG residents. Dividends on these shares are not subject to the withholding tax.

rate determined by the formula $r = 0.70 - \dfrac{N}{P}$, where P is taxable income, and N is A\$32 million in 1974, but adjusted with increased capital expenditures in subsequent years.[18] Thus, if taxable income is A\$100 million and N = A\$32 million, the tax rate of 38 percent would apply, and the tax would be A\$38 million. In addition, the government would receive a 20 percent dividend on its shares plus the 15 percent withholding tax on dividends paid to foreign shareholders. This would give the government a total revenue of A\$58 million. It will be noted from Table 15 that this amount is slightly less than what the government would receive on the same amount of net earnings under the original tax regime following the period of accelerated depreciation and the tax holiday. On the other hand, if BCL's net before-tax earnings were A\$162 million (as shown in Table 12), government receipts (excluding royalties and customs duties) would have been A\$107 million in 1983 under the new tax regime, as contrasted with A\$96 million under the tax regime provided in the original agreement. Thus, under the new tax regime the government would receive a smaller amount from BCL operations when earnings are relatively low but a substantially larger amount when they are relatively high.

PNG Government Outlays
Related to BCL

PNG government outlays related to the Bougainville mine may be divided into three categories: (1) outlays for the purchase of BCL equity shares; (2) capital outlays for infrastructure related to the mining communities, etc.; and (3) additional current expenditures related to public services. The latter item is difficult to project and is, in any case, offset by income from electric power, telecommunications, and local taxes not included in the sources of PNG government income shown in Table 14. The fiscal impact of the first two outlays (items 1 and 2) is complicated by the fact that the PNG government borrowed A\$25 million to finance the purchase of the equity shares and another A\$20 million to finance the capital outlays for the town of Arawa and is therefore obligated to make debt service payments on the loans. These outlays and receipts are summarized in Table 16, together with a calculation of net payments for the period 1969–91. The projected capital outlays terminate after 1975, but debt service payments continue until the loans are repaid in 1995. Net payments were highest

---

[18] The 1974 agreement had not been published at the time of writing, and the information regarding the new tax regime was derived from an unofficial text.

Table 16. Projected PNG Government Capital Outlays and Borrowings Related to the Bougainville Mine
(millions of Australian dollars)

Calendar year	Equity				Other				Total net payment
	Equity payments	Borrowing^a	Loan repayment and interest	Net payment	Expenditures	Borrowings^b	Loan repayment and interest	Net payment	
1969	—	—	—	—	9.0	—	—	9.0	9.0
1970	18.75	18.75	—	—	5.0	2.0	—	3.0	3.0
1971	6.25	6.25	1.0	1.0	13.0	12.0	—	1.0	2.0
1972	1.0	—	2.0	3.0	9.0	6.0	—	3.0	6.0
1973	0.5	—	1.5	2.0	1.0	—	—	1.0	3.0
1974	—	—	1.5	1.5	3.0	—	1.5	4.5	6.0
1975	—	—	1.5	1.5	1.0	—	3.0	4.0	5.5
1976	—	—	1.5	1.5	—	—	3.0	3.0	4.5
1977	—	—	1.5	1.5	—	—	4.0	4.0	5.5
1978	—	—	1.5	1.5	—	—	3.0	3.0	4.5
1979	—	—	1.5	1.5	—	—	3.0	3.0	4.5
1980	—	—	1.5	1.5	—	—	3.0	3.0	4.5
1981	—	—	1.5	1.5	—	—	3.0	3.0	4.5
1982	—	—	1.5	1.5	—	—	4.0	4.0	5.5
1983	—	—	1.5	1.5	—	—	3.0	3.0	4.5
1984	—	—	1.5	1.5	—	—	1.5	1.5	3.0
1985	—	—	3.0	3.0	—	—	—	—	3.0
1986	—	—	3.0	3.0	—	—	—	—	3.0
1987	—	—	2.0	2.0	—	—	—	—	2.0
1988	—	—	3.0	3.0	—	—	—	—	3.0
1989	—	—	3.0	3.0	—	—	—	—	3.0
1990	—	—	3.0	3.0	—	—	—	—	3.0
1991	—	—	13.0^c	13.0	—	—	—	—	13.0

Source: BCL.

a A$25 million of PNG equity from Australian loans at 7¾ percent, repayable 1985–95.
b A$20 million Arawa loan at 6⅞ percent, repayable with interest 1974–84 in semiannual payments of $1,593 million.
c A$13 million equals estimated 1991 residual value of outstanding repayments.

during the construction period, but after 1975 are limited to service payments on the loans.

Prior to 1972 net payments by the PNG government, summarized in Table 16, exceeded direct revenues from BCL, but in 1972 they were approximately equal, and in 1973 estimated payments were A$3 million as against revenues from BCL of A$34.6 million (see Table 14). Payments on the loans continue until 1995, but they constitute only a small percentage of projected receipts.

EMPLOYMENT AND TRAINING

Although at the peak of construction in 1971 over 10,000 workers were employed in the development of the Bougainville mine, normal employment for the mine is about 3,600. In December 1973, total manpower employed directly by BCL was 3,844, of which 2,915 (76 percent) were indigenes. This included 452 indigenous apprentices and trainees. In addition, 1,171 indigenes and 190 expatriates were employed by construction contractors and service facilities directly associated with the mine. Employment in the mine is a small percentage of the adult male population of Bougainville (21,000, as of June 1971). The normal work force of the mine of 3,600 is composed of 900 subprofessionals and skilled administrators; 570 subprofessional and skilled mobile equipment operators; 550 subprofessional and skilled static plant operators; 790 subprofessional and trades, engineer, and maintenance employees; 670 low-skilled employees; and 120 professional and top-management personnel.

Table 17 shows the actual percentage of indigenous workers in each skill category in 1972, as well as the company's localization targets for 1975 and 1980.

PNG had no readily available national pool of skilled and semi-skilled manpower, and virtually all skilled and semiskilled labor had to be trained by the company. For this task, BCL established a Mine Training Centre at the mine, an apprenticeship program under the direction of the Centre, and a scholarship program for students to attend the University of PNG, the Institute of Technology, and other colleges throughout PNG. A total of 145 scholarships were awarded in 1972.

By the end of 1972, BCL had trained nearly 2,000 equipment operators, about 500 plant operators, 360 maintenance workers, 265 administrative personnel, 11 professionals, and 3 subprofessionals. To achieve the localization goals indicated above, the Mine Training

Table 17. Percentage of Indigenous Workers in Each Skill Category, as of 1972, and as Projected for 1975 and 1980

Skill category	1972	1975	1980
Managerial and professional	1	2	46
Subprofessional	4	10	65
Supervisory and skilled	36	52	82
Semiskilled	95	100	100
Unskilled	100	100	100
All workers	70	78	91

Source: BCL.

Centre will train several thousand additional operators, maintenance workers, and administrative and supervisory personnel over the 1973–75 period, and provide several hundred scholarships for professional and subprofessional education. The magnitude and comprehensiveness of the program are unique among the world's mine training programs.

BCL has an extensive apprenticeship program covering such important trades as auto/diesel mechanic, heavy-equipment fitter, machinist fitter, electrical fitter/mechanic, plumber/drainer, carpenter/joiner, metal fabricator welder, refrigerator mechanic, instrument mechanic, auto electrician, linesman, panel beater, painter/decorator, power station operator, and mechanical equipment operator. In 1972 there were 241 apprentices who were in training or had completed training during the year, and an estimated 380 were in the apprenticeship program for 1973. The BCL apprenticeship program operates under the PNG government Apprenticeship Board and establishes regulations for the granting of certificates to workers in specific trades.

As of 1971 there were 1,674 Papua New Guineans registered under the PNG Apprenticeship System,[19] and in 1972, 372 workers completed their apprenticeships,[20] of which less than 300 were in the technical and mechanical fields (excluding clerks, hairdressers, printers, bakers, etc.). In 1972 an estimated 95 apprentices in the BCL apprenticeship training program had completed their apprenticeships, all of which were in the mechanical or technical fields. Thus it appears that the BCL apprenticeship program accounts for a substantial proportion of all PNG apprenticeship trainees.[21]

Actually, far more workers must be trained by BCL than will be employed in the mine at any given time if the targets are to be met. This is true because of the high rate of turnover of the mine em-

---

[19] Commonwealth of Australia, *Papua New Guinea Report for 1970–71* (Canberra: Commonwealth of Australia, 1972), p. 148.
[20] Information from PNG Manpower Planning Unit, July 1973.
[21] Information from the BCL Mine Training Centre.

ployees. Over the period June 1, 1972–May 31, 1973, the average work force in the nonstaff category was 2,650. During this period there were 1,125 terminations. In the skilled and semiskilled group, terminations during the year amounted to over 35 percent of the work force. This means that 700–800 trained and experienced workers left the mine, many of whom will eventually employ their skills in other sectors of the PNG economy. Even the nonskilled laborers will have acquired an understanding of the disciplines of a modern industrial society. It seems likely, therefore, that over the years BCL will make a significant contribution to the supply of mechanics, electricians, machinists, welders, heavy-equipment operators, carpenters, and supervisors in the PNG economy.

Although the company is obligated under the agreement to replace expatriate workers with indigenes as rapidly as is feasible, the company also has a strong monetary incentive to do so. The training programs cost an estimated A$1.5 million per year, but when the company has achieved its localization target of replacing some 900 expatriate employees with Papua New Guineans, there will be an annual saving in the neighborhood of A$5 million per year.[22] Total wages, salaries, and supplements were estimated to be in excess of A$26 million in 1973, of which about two-thirds are paid to non-indigenous employees. But this ratio will gradually shift, so that by 1990 less than one-third of the wages will go to nonindigenous employees.

CONTRIBUTION OF THE MINE TO DOMESTIC PRODUCTION

Domestic purchases of goods and services by BCL were estimated to be about A$4 million in 1973, rising to an estimated A$20 million in 1980.[23] About 40 percent of the value of these domestic purchases is direct import content. However, apart from agricultural products, domestic value added in these purchases consists mainly of services, such as transport and distribution (including the services of importing firms) and utilities. A high proportion of BCL's domestic purchases are

[22] The difference in annual remuneration between an expatriate and an indigene averages about A$5,000 per year. In addition, recruiting and moving costs of an expatriate involve an outlay of A$5,000 during the first year of employment. Partly offsetting this, however, is the high absenteeism of indigenous workers (averaging about 25 percent). Because of the high rate of turnover among indigenous workers, the training program will have to be maintained.

[23] The 1980 estimate is from the Scott report.

made in Bougainville. Purchases of domestic industrial products constitute only a small percentage of the total. Since there is not likely to be a substantial amount of industrialization in Bougainville in the foreseeable future, domestic production stimulated by purchases of BCL and its employees is likely to be confined largely to locally consumed agricultural products, transport, wholesaling and retailing (mainly of imported goods), construction, lumber and sawmill products, repairing, and miscellaneous consumer-oriented service industries.

BCL is seeking to promote investment and productivity in each of these activities. In addition to an agricultural program designed to promote production of locally consumed vegetables, poultry, fruit, and livestock, BCL has played an active role in establishing the Panguna Development Foundation Ltd. (PDF). Designed to encourage indigenous enterprise, PDF has provided direct assistance to a number of local firms. An affiliate of PDF, PDF Holdings Ltd., acts as a holding company for various commercial enterprises, including Arawa Enterprises Ltd., which operates a supermarket and a department store in Arawa; Barapinang Enterprises Ltd., which operates a supermarket and tavern in Panguna; and PDF Wholesale Pty. Ltd., which acts as a buying agent and provides warehouse facilities for several local stores. The company has indicated its intention to offer shares in these enterprises to local Bougainvillians, and such shares provide a means of channeling a portion of the payments made by BCL to the landowners into local enterprise. The firms provide employment for several hundred Bougainvillians and reduce prices to local consumers by providing an efficient distribution system for local and imported goods.

Backward and Forward Linkages

The material inputs of the Bougainville mine are in large part the products of a modern industrial and agricultural economy. Just how fast the domestic value added of BCL purchases will rise depends upon the character of PNG's agricultural and industrial development. In the immediate future, production of food required by the commissaries of the mine may represent the most important prospect for backward linkage. However, BCL's purchases of foodstuffs are small compared with the total PNG demand for these commodities that are now largely imported. There are only a few industrial products in demand by BCL which are both potentially suitable for production in PNG in the foreseeable future and are purchased by BCL in sufficient quantities to have a significant impact on the total market.

Industries for producing three of these products, namely, explosives, grinding balls, and hydrated lime, have been under consideration.[24] There are other products such as cement that are purchased in significant quantities by the Bougainville mine, but the amounts are not large enough to be a deciding factor in the establishment of the industry.[25]

As regards forward linkages, even copper wire production and other copper-fabricating industries would not use inputs from BCL until a smelter and refinery have been established. Although a smelter and refinery may one day be established in PNG, there were several reasons for deciding to export concentrates rather than blister or refined copper. One was that at the time the mine was under consideration it was believed it would be difficult, if not impossible, to obtain long-term contracts for refined copper, while BCL was able to obtain contracts for up to fifteen years for copper concentrates. A second reason was the effect of a prospective smelter on the population and environment of Bougainville. Third, the building of a smelter and refinery would have greatly increased the initial investment requirements of the project. And, finally, a market would have been needed for acid by-products. Since the Bougainville mine was established some of these factors, such as the ability to market refined copper, have changed.[26] Moreover, the prospect of a copper mine at Ok Tedi in northwestern Papua increases the likelihood that a copper smelter and refinery will become feasible.

[24] See R. Kent Wilson and W. Irlam, *Import Analysis and Prospective Industry Study: Papua New Guinea* (Melbourne: Australian Government Department of External Territories, 1972), p. 72.
[25] For an analysis of these prospective industries, see ibid., pp. 32–73.
[26] Ibid., p. 73.

9
Financial Returns to BCL Equity Investors: A Simulation Analysis

As was pointed out in Chapter 6, the project initiators, Conzinc Riotinto of Australia Ltd. and New Broken Hill Consolidated Ltd. (CRA–NBHC), began making cash outlays for exploration and evaluation of the ore deposit in 1964, but no dividends were received until 1973. Although we do not have a complete year-by-year breakdown of these outlays, we know that A$21.4 million was expended from about mid-1964 to mid-1969 when the final decision was made to construct the mine. During the year ending June 1970, the project initiators made cash outlays of A$28 million, and during the period July 1970–December 31, 1971, there were additional cash outlays of A$24 million, or A$73.4 million in all. However, NBHC was dissolved in 1972, and its shares in BCL distributed to its stockholders, which included CRA.[1] CRA also sold some of its shares at a premium to general public investors so that CRA's net equity contribution for the entire period up to the beginning of operations was A$56 million. (The par value of CRA's equity is A$71.7 million, or 53.6 percent of the total par value of the shares amounting to A$133.7 million.) All of these financial transactions complicate the analysis of the cash flow to CRA's equity, as well as to that of the general public stockholders who have acquired their shares at various prices. Included among the public stockholders are the original stockholders of NBHC, the internal rate of return on whose equity will be similar to that on CRA's equity.

---

[1] Actually, the shares were held in Bougainville Mining Ltd. (BML), which held 80 percent of the shares in BCPL, the remainder being held by the PNG government.

Nevertheless, we have lumped all general public stockholders together and given as their cash outflow the aggregate initial cost of the shares as issued without seeking to differentiate among them in terms of what each category actually paid for its shares.

Cash outlays by the PNG government for its 20 percent equity shareholding were reported to be A$18.75 million in 1970, A$6.25 million in 1971, A$1 million in 1972, and A$500,000 in 1973—or A$26.5 million in total. PNG paid for its equity investment largely out of an A$25 million loan from the Australian government repayable at $7\frac{3}{4}$ percent interest over the period 1985–95. However, we shall ignore the means of financing PNG's equity investment and count the total investment as cash outflow. Cash inflow will consist of dividends and withholding taxes on dividends paid to nonresidents. For purposes of analyzing PNG's internal rate of return on its investment in BCL, we shall ignore corporate taxes and other sources of income related to the operations of the Bougainville mine. It might be noted, however, that had the PNG government not owned a 20 percent share of BCL, tax revenues would have been higher.

Since dividends have only been paid out of earnings for 1972–73, we lack an appropriate period for determining the internal rates of return to the three categories of equity investors. Dividend payments out of profits for the calendar year 1973 (payable in April 1974) were A$36.5 million to CRA; A$18.2 million to the general public stockholders; A$25.5 million to the PNG government, including the withholding tax on dividends to foreign residents.[2] Given the uncertainties regarding future copper and gold prices, it would be hazardous to project dividend payments beyond 1973. BCL's net earnings in 1973 (A$158.4 million) were certainly high in terms of past expectations. The average price for copper sold by BCL during 1973 was about 87 U.S. cents per pound, and the average price received for gold was about U.S.$97 per ounce. Although the sharp increases in the prices of copper and gold in the first half of 1974 will mean higher net earnings for the year, the drastic decline in copper prices in the fall of 1974 suggests that BCL's net earnings will decline substantially in 1975. Meanwhile, operating costs rose by about 20 percent in the first half of 1974 over the corresponding period in 1973, and are likely to continue to reflect the rise in world prices. In addition, BCL's copper production is scheduled to decline from the 183,000 metric tons produced during 1973 as the grade of ore decreases. Thus the odds appear

---

[2] Data on dividends to CRA and the public shareholders are after payment of the 15 percent withholding tax.

to favor a decline in BCL's average before-tax net earnings over the next decade as compared with those for 1973.

In 1973 BCL declared A$80.2 million in cash dividends, of which A$36.5 million (after withholding taxes) went to CRA, A$18.1 million went to the public shareholders (excluding withholding taxes on foreign shareholders), and A$25.5 million went to the PNG government (including receipts from withholding taxes). BCL's net earnings in 1973 were A$158.4 million, but this amount included an A$13.8 million exchange gain and reflected a deduction of A$18.5 million in financing charges.[3] Loan payments, including prepayments, totaling A$68 million were made out of earnings during 1973. In order to illustrate the effects of the 1974 agreement on dividends received by shareholders after 1973, I shall assume that before-tax earnings after 1973 are A$162 million each year, and that A$35 million per year is used to retire the external debt until the debt is repaid at the end of 1978. It will also be assumed that net capital expenditures are exactly equal to depreciation charges. Under these assumptions the corporate tax in 1974, and thereafter through 1978, is approximately A$82 million and after-tax earnings, A$80 million. After debt payments of A$35 million per year, A$45 million is available for dividends, of which A$21.0 million accrues to CRA (after withholding taxes), A$10.2 million to the public shareholders (after withholding taxes), and A$13.8 million to the PNG government (including withholding tax receipts). Beginning in 1979 funds available for dividends increase to A$80 million, of which A$36.5 million is paid to CRA, A$18.1 million to the public shareholders, and A$25.4 million to the PNG government (including withholding tax receipts). The results of this simulation are shown in Table 18.

On the basis of the simulation of cash flow to equity stockholders, shown in Table 18, internal rates of return over a fifteen-year production period through 1986 are as follows: CRA, 25.4 percent; public shareholders, 21.5 percent; and the PNG government, 41.8 percent. If we were to include the government's corporate tax receipts of A$82 million in its cash flow, the internal rate of return to the PNG government is 86 percent.

---

[3] Financing charges are mainly interest on debt but are offset in part by interest earned on balances held. Interest paid on outstanding debt declined to about A$12 million in 1974 and will continue to decline as the debt is paid off. On the other hand, interest paid on loans in 1974 was almost entirely offset by interest earned on working balances. For data on 1973 operations, see *Bougainville Copper Ltd. Annual Report 1973* (Melbourne: BCL, 1974).

Table 18. Simulation of Cash Flow to Equity Stockholders in BCL
(millions of Australian dollars)

Calendar year	CRA	Public shareholders	PNG government[a]	
			1	2
1964	(1.0)	—	—	—
1965	(2.0)	—	—	—
1966	(3.0)	—	—	—
1967	(3.0)	—	—	—
1968	(3.0)	—	—	—
1969	(4.3)	—	—	—
1970	(21.8)	—	(18.75)	(18.75)
1971	(17.9)	(51.2)	(6.25)	(6.25)
1972	4.9	2.4	2.66[b]	2.66[b]
1973	36.5	18.1	25.0[b]	25.0[b]
1974	21.0	10.2	13.8	95.8
1975	21.0	10.2	13.8	95.8
1976	21.0	10.2	13.8	95.8
1977	21.0	10.2	13.8	95.8
1978	21.0	10.2	13.8	95.8
1979	36.5	18.1	25.4	107.4
1980	36.5	18.1	25.4	107.4
1981	36.5	18.1	25.4	107.4
1982	36.5	18.1	25.4	107.4
1983	36.5	18.1	25.4	107.4
1984	36.5	18.1	25.4	107.4
1985	36.5	18.1	25.4	107.4
1986	36.5	18.1	25.4	107.4
Internal rates of return through 1986[c]	25.4	21.5	41.8	86.0

Sources: Data through 1973 from BCL. Data beginning with 1974 have been simulated on the basis of assumptions given in text.

Notes:

Cash inflow data are for dividends declared on earnings for year indicated and not for year dividends were paid.

Numbers in parentheses indicate cash outflow in millions of Australian dollars.

[a] Includes withholding taxes on dividends paid to nonresidents. Column 1 excludes corporate taxes while column 2 includes corporate taxes.

[b] Adjusted for payments on PNG equity of A$1 million and A$500,000 in 1972 and 1973, respectively.

[c] No allowance made for liquidation value of stockholders' equity.

The cash flow simulation, shown in Table 18, is probably unrealistic, since it assumes a continuation of CRA's 1973 earnings based on an average price of copper of 87 U.S. cents per pound. I have, therefore, undertaken another simulation with BCL's earnings based on 97 U.S. cents-per-pound copper in 1974 but declining to 60 U.S. cents per pound in 1975 and remaining at this level every year through

1986.[4] (BCL's receipts from gold production are assumed to remain at the 1974 level, and operating costs are also assumed to continue at the 1974 level.) Under these assumptions, CRA's internal rate of return over the fifteen-year production period through 1986 is 22.8 percent, and the return to the public shareholders is 17.2 percent. It should be noted that actual returns may be substantially lower if the price of copper were to average no more than 60 U.S. cents per pound and operating costs continue to rise in response to world inflation.

One of the difficulties in calculating rates of return over a period of fifteen to twenty years is that the calculations are made in current rather than constant dollars. The Australian consumer price index increased by a compound rate of over 7 percent between 1969 (the year construction of the mine began) and 1973, and in 1973 prices were increasing at a rate in excess of 10 percent per annum. Thus, on the basis of 1973 dollars, capital outlays by CRA, which began in 1964 and continued through 1971, are substantially understated, while future returns in constant dollars may be substantially overstated. If future dividends were to rise with the general rise in prices, the error would be partly compensated, but we have not made this assumption in our simulation. For example, the simulated figure of A$36.5 million for dividend payments to CRA in 1983 would have a value of about A$18.2 million in 1973 dollars, assuming a 7 percent rate of inflation, and only A$14.2 million, assuming a 10 percent rate of inflation. A rough calculation indicates that in 1973 dollars the internal rates of return for CRA, given in Table 18 and in the preceding paragraph, would be reduced by nearly one-third, assuming a 10 percent annual increase in prices after 1973.

[4] Under the 1974 agreement the tax formula applicable to BCL earnings during the first half of 1974 differs from that to be applied after July 1, 1974, but owing to the lack of data I have assumed that the new formula to be applied after that date is employed with respect to the projected net earnings for the entire year.

10
Renegotiating the Bougainville Mine Agreement

From the time the Bougainville mine went into operation there were strong demands in PNG for a renegotiation of the Bougainville mining agreement, and despite the fact that the mine had been in operation for only two years, renegotiations were initiated in the spring of 1974. Some PNG politicians argue that the agreement was much too favorable to BCL at the time it was negotiated, while others feel that, although the agreement may have been proper at the time it was negotiated in 1967, conditions have changed so it is no longer "fair" or "equitable," and its provisions should be altered in favor of the government. Some PNG government officials take the position that the new self-governing state is neither legally nor morally bound by agreements made by the Australian government and that the PNG government has the right to demand a renegotiation on its own terms.[1] The high level of BCL's earnings for 1973 heightened the demands for a renegotiation of the agreement, particularly with a view to shortening the period during which BCL had no corporate tax obligation. It is not the purpose of this study to pass judgment on the fairness of the agreement or on the desirability of a renegotiation of the terms. However, a brief review and analysis of the major proposals for renegotiation, together with a brief summary of the outcome, may suggest some lessons for the negotiation of future mine development agreements.

---

[1] In the opinion of a legal advisor with a leading international agency, the PNG government is legally bound by the agreement. A unilateral change in the terms of the agreement would constitute a violation of international law with possible serious consequences for future investment in PNG.

PRELIMINARY PROPOSALS
FOR RENEGOTIATION

Prior to June 1974 there was no agreed PNG government position either on what the government should seek in the course of a renegotiation of the agreement or what tactics should be employed. A wide range of proposals were voiced by members of the PNG House of Assembly, ranging from the acquisition of majority equity ownership plus the imposition of an effective tax rate of 80 percent, to minor adjustments in the tax regime that would give the PNG government some additional revenue. The broad categories of proposals for changes in the Bougainville mine agreement emanating from PNG politicians may be summarized as follows:

1. Adjusting the tax provisions to give the PNG government larger revenues immediately and a larger share of future revenues.
2. Increasing the PNG government's share of the equity in BCL.
3. Requiring BCL to make a commitment for the achievement of specified goals for replacing expatriate workers with PNG citizens.
4. Requiring BCL to establish a smelter and/or a refinery at some future date to be determined by negotiation.
5. Increasing PNG government control over company policies by requiring that certain decisions be approved by the government's representatives on the BCL board of directors.

In preparation for possible future negotiations, the PNG government commissioned several studies of the agreement by outside consultants. Although the reports of the consultants have not been officially published, some have been made available to the press and given rather general circulation. The most comprehensive report is that of Professor Louis T. Wells, Jr., of the Harvard Graduate School of Business, which was presented to the PNG government in September 1973. Wells's principal recommendations relating to taxation were (1) the introduction of accelerated depreciation (Division 10) deductions concurrently with the three-year tax holiday instead of following the tax holiday period as provided in the present agreement; and (2) the elimination of the provision in the old Section 33 of the Australian Income Tax Ordinance exempting 20 percent of the net earnings of BCL from income taxation. The latter provision would increase the 50 percent rate on taxable income from a 40 percent effective rate under the present agreement to a full 50 percent effective rate. Both recommendations clearly violate the 1967 agreement and could be applied only with the consent of the company without a legal violation of the agreement.

The second recommendation involves a value judgment as to the fairness of the division of the rents as between 40–60 and 50–50 (excluding the government's own dividend receipts and the dividend withholding tax). However, the first recommendation involves an important principle of taxation. The purpose of both the tax holiday and the accelerated depreciation was to allow the company to pay off its indebtedness and recoup its equity investment before being subject to a tax on earnings. Wells argued that the application of accelerated depreciation *following* the tax holiday is redundant, since accelerated depreciation alone would provide for the retirement of the debt and the recovery of the equity investment before taxation. However, there is another aspect of the problem. For an investment to be attractive, the company cannot expect to employ its entire cash flow for debt retirement and the return of its equity over a period of years. If this were to require six or seven years and all cash flow were applied to debt retirement and recovery of equity outlays plus necessary capital outlays over the period, the internal rate of return to equity over the period would be zero. The company, of course, did not expect the present high earnings during the early years of operation, but made its investment decision on the expectation of a volume of cash flow over a period of eight years of income free of taxes which would allow debt retirement, equity recoupment, and necessary capital expenditures, plus an allowance for dividends sufficient to provide a reasonable rate of return on the equity investment. If the 1973 level of earnings were to continue beyond the period of debt retirement and capital recoupment, it could be argued that the company could have paid a 40 or 50 percent corporate tax beginning with the fourth year of operations (following the tax holiday concurrently with accelerated depreciation) and still provide enough dividends for an attractive rate of return. But this could not have been known in advance, and we come back to the issue of what is an appropriate division of the rents between the company and the government. However, the point to be made here is that it is not sufficient from the standpoint of attracting investment to permit debt retirement and capital recovery alone over the first several years of operations; it is necessary to provide for a reasonable internal rate of return to the equity investment as well.

Wells's other major recommendation was that the company commit itself to specific localization targets for 1975, 1980, and 1985, covering the categories of skilled workers, subprofessional and supervisory personnel, and managerial and professional personnel. (Currently, unskilled and semiskilled positions are occupied almost completely by PNG citizens.) Wells's recommended localization targets are virtually the same as those established by the company, so the principal issue here is whether the company should bind itself to these targets, possibly at the cost of operational efficiency. It would appear that this issue could be satisfactorily compromised, since the government shares the company's interest in maximizing efficiency and, hence, revenues. A major question that might arise would be whether the company's training program was adequate to achieve the localization targets. This might be dealt with by a joint BCL–PNG government commission (with one outside member to cast the deciding vote in case of a tie) to review and provide surveillance over the localization program.

Wells also considered the issue of increased PNG government ownership, which he regards as primarily an emotional or political issue. According to Wells, only in the event that the political appeal of a larger PNG ownership proved to be overwhelming should the government insist on the right to acquire additional shares in BCL. In this event he suggests that the acquisition should take place gradually over a number of years at a price based on the market price of the shares.

In his report Wells casts doubt on the desirability of establishing smelting and refining facilities in the immediate future, although he suggests that the government require the company to submit information for a feasibility study.

A report to the PNG government prepared by Professor Anthony Clunies Ross of the University of Papua New Guinea and Dr. Ross Garnaut of the Australian National University included a proposal for a graduated scale of taxation on profits in excess of a "fair return to the investor." However, the proposed tax is not a straightforward excess profits tax. It involves a complicated formula that approximates a tax that would prevent the internal rate of return to equity from exceeding a level believed necessary to attract a mining firm to make the investment. There is perhaps some merit in negotiating a mine contract that provides for an adjustment in the tax rate, say, after ten years of operation, in the event that the internal rate of return exceeds an agreed minimum. However, I do not believe that tax adjustments can properly be made on an annual basis from the beginning of profitable operations. Mineral prices fluctuate so widely that a provision for frequent adjustments in the tax rate would introduce great uncertainty for the investor and would certainly reduce the attractiveness of an investment in a developing country.

RENEGOTIATION OF THE
1967 AGREEMENT

Serious negotiations on a revision of the 1967 agreement began with the submission of the company's proposal in early June 1974, followed by the formal submission of a PNG government proposal shortly thereafter. Fortunately for the progress of the negotiations, the details of the proposals were not made public so the government negotiators did not become publicly committed to positions from which they would find it politically difficult to retreat. Initially the proposals, as they related to taxes on BCL, were quite far apart, and at one point negotiations nearly broke down. The new tax formula, as summarized in Chapter 8, in effect provided for a $33\frac{1}{3}$ percent tax on earnings up to A\$87 million, or A\$29 million, plus a 70 percent tax on earnings above A\$87 million. This means, in effect, that the company will be able to earn A\$57 million after taxes (or 15 percent of A\$390 million adjusted for future additions to capital investment) provided its before-tax income is at least A\$87 million.

The 1974 agreement also provides some unique ways for dealing with the effects of future inflation on the real rate of return and the effects of the foreign exchange value of the PNG currency on earnings should the currency become overvalued by as much as 15 percent (in terms of the "effective" exchange rate in relation to the dollar). In such cases appropriate adjustments are to be made in the tax rates, as determined by consultations between the PNG government and the company. The new agreement also provides that any increase in the dividend withholding tax in excess of 15 percent of gross dividends payable to nonresidents of PNG is to be matched by a corresponding reduction in the amount of tax paid by the company, provided that the amount payable by the company will not be reduced below the amount payable under the normal company tax. Finally, both the tax holiday and the accelerated depreciation provisions of the 1967 agreement are eliminated. However, special arrangements were agreed upon for deferring a portion of the company's tax liability for the years 1975, 1976, and 1977 in order to assure that the company would be able to undertake the amount of capital expenditure necessary to maintain the current level of metal production.

In addition to the revision of the tax regime, the 1974 agreement contains certain provisions relating to the social and environmental impact of the company's operations, and provides that the company will pay to the PNG government 50 U.S. cents per ton of contained copper sold to be transferred by the government to the Bougainville Non-Renewable Resource Fund. The 1974 agreement also makes special provision for the development of certain areas not now under development but included in the original BCL lease. When the government decides that the development of these areas may proceed, it will grant a special mining lease and will have the right to take up a majority beneficial interest in a separate company formed to develop these areas. Other salient features of the new agreement include provisions for its review and possible renegotiation every seven years, and a new arbitration procedure for dealing with disputes. Under the latter, where the parties are unable to agree upon a third arbitrator, the third arbitrator will be appointed by the Supreme Court of Papua New Guinea from an international panel chosen by the PNG government and the company.

I will not attempt to judge the fairness of the October 1974 agreement, which at the time of writing was not ratified by either the PNG House of Assembly or by the shareholders of BCL. There are many desirable features in the agreement, including the minimum tax on earnings up to 15 percent of an agreed asset value of the company; and the provisions for adjustment in the tax formula in the likely event of substantial erosion of real returns from inflation and the possibility of the impairment of the company's income from an overvalued exchange rate for the PNG currency. On the other hand, the government's demand for renegotiation was made at a time when copper prices were abnormally high and by the time the new agreement was reached the LME price had fallen by more than half from its 1974 high. Clearly, two years' experience under the original 1967 agreement, which was generally considered fair at the time it was negotiated (even by the PNG officials who later demanded its renegotiation), is not sufficient time to judge the appropriateness of a tax arrangement. The 1974 agreement apparently cuts the return to the private shareholders in 1974 to less than 40 percent of what they would have received under the original agreement, and by about half of what they would have received if the average price of copper had been 60 U.S. cents per pound during 1974. At the time of writing, the LME copper price is under 60 U.S. cents per pound, and BCL's costs rose by about 20 percent between mid-1973 and mid-1974. Given the large debt payments, BCL's financial return could well be too low for dividend payments for the next two or three years. Reserves from years of high profitability should be accumulated to compensate for low cash flow in lean years. If host governments adopt the principle that foreign investors may make no more than "reasonable profits" in good years so that there is no carry-over in periods when profits are low or nonexistent, high-risk investment in the mineral industry in developing countries is not likely to prove attractive to foreign companies. Renegotiation of mine development agreements should not take place sooner than five years after the beginning of commercial operations or until the debt has been retired, whichever is longer, and such renegotiations should be subject to guidelines relating to minimum levels of after-tax earnings or minimum internal rates of return projected over the life of the agreement.

Appendix A
The Calculation of the Internal Rate of Return

Assume that a project is expected to take six years to construct and is expected to yield returns for fifteen years after it has begun operations. Let us denote the expenditures $X_1, X_2, \ldots, X_6$ and the returns $Y_1, Y_2, \ldots, Y_{15}$ in the order in which they occur. The internal rate of return is that rate of interest which, when used to discount the receipt stream and compound the expenditure stream, yields the same present value for the two streams. Denoting present value of expenditures as $(PV)_x$ and present value of receipts as $(PV)_y$, and r as the internal rate of return,

$$(PV)_x = X_1(1+r)^5 + X_2(1+r)^4 + X_3(1+r)^3 + X_4(1+r)^2 + X_5(1+r) + X_6$$

$$(PV)_y = \frac{Y_1}{(1+r)} + \frac{Y_2}{(1+r)^2} + \ldots + \frac{Y_{15}}{(1+r)^{15}}$$

$$(PV)_x = (PV)_y$$

When r is greater than zero, the present value of the expenditures is greater than the sum of the expenditures, and the present value of the receipts is less than the sum of the receipts.

Appendix B
Comparison of Agreements for Projects in Indonesia, Botswana, and Papua New Guinea

Table B-1. Summary of Terms of Three Project Agreements

	Ertsberg Mine	Selebi-Pikwe Mine	Bougainville Mine
Date of contract and project locations	1967, located at 11,500 feet in Mount Cartensz, Irian	1972, Botswana	1967, Bougainville Island, Panguna, PNG
Project agreement parties	Government of Indonesia and Freeport of Indonesia	Government of Botswana and Botswana RST Ltd. (BRST). BRST owns 85% of project and is owned by Anglo-American Group (30%); American Metal Climax (30%); and public shareholders (40%)	Government of PNG and Bougainville Copper Pty. Ltd., which is owned 20% by government of PNG; 60% (indirectly) by CRA, NBHC, and public shareholders
Production and finance	65,000 tons of copper in concentrates per annum Equity: U.S. $23 million Loan: U.S. $112 million	17,000 tons of nickel in matte per annum; 15,500 tons of copper in matte per annum; and 127,500 tons of sulfur	150,000–180,000 tons of copper concentrates; 500,000 ounces of gold. Equity: A$130 million Loan: A$280 million
Government contributions	None (?)	Infrastructure approximately U.S. $80 million	Government infrastructure A$4 million; government equity 20% at par A$26 million
Taxes and royalties	Tax: years 4–10: 35% of profit or 50% of net sales. Year 10: 41.75% of profits or 10% of net sales No royalties	Tax: 40% of net income plus 1% for each 1% by which profit exceeds 48.5% up to maximum of 65% Royalty of 7.5% net operating income or minimum of U.S. $750,000 per annum	Tax: 3-year holiday followed by accelerated write-off of fixed assets. Thereafter, tax to rise from general company rate to 50% over 4 years, then remains constant until year 25, after which it increases by 1% per annum to maximum of 66% Royalty 1.25% of f.o.b. Dividend withholding tax, 15%; import levy, 2.5%; land rates, local rate

Incentives/write-offs	3-year tax holiday. Equipment and supplies for project exempt from import duty. Accelerated write-offs of fixed assets	Accelerated depreciation	20% of income from copper and gold is tax-exempt. 3-year tax holiday. Accelerated depreciation of fixed assets
Local participation	None provided for in agreement	Government of Botswana has 15% of equity free	Government of PNG has 20% of equity (at par). Indirect through Bougainville Copper Pty. Ltd.: Panguna Foundation, 0.9%; PNG public shareholders, 0.6%
Notes	Local work force to 75% of total after 8 years. Investment (equity and loan) insured under U.S. and West German official programs	Government of Botswana has loans for infrastructure from IBRD and agencies in Canada, United Kingdom, United States. German and South African agencies provided loans to Botswana RST. Loans guaranteed by private firms. U.S. OPIC guarantee of equity	Company undertakes to mount staff training scheme, favor local suppliers, and examine feasibility of processing.

Source: Based on G. O. Gutman, "Objectives, Strategy and Tactics in Mining Projects with Reference to Bougainville Copper," paper delivered at the Seventh Waigani Seminar on Law and Development in Melanesia, held at the University of Papua New Guinea, April 29–May 4, 1973 (see Annex A).

Index

Accelerated depreciation, xx, 7, 8, 9, 10, 18, 23, 29, 129; Bougainville project, 9, 32, 84, 98, 113–114, 128, 129

Accounting rate of return, 5, 75, 76, 77

Allende, Salvador, 19

American Smelting and Refining Company (ASARCO), Toquepala project, xix, 40–44, 46, 47, 58, 59–61, 62–65

Amortization allowance, 11, 12; Toquepala project, 45, 46, 70, 75. *See also* Capital consumption allowance; Depletion; Depreciation.

Anaconda Copper, Chilean holdings, 19, 99

Arawa, Papua New Guinea, 85, 102, 115

Arawa Enterprises Ltd., 120

Arbitration, 27, 88, 132

Australia, BCP mining agreement, 80–82, 86–88; Bougainville project, xix, 95, 96, 98–99; loans, 85–86, 123; PNG administration, 78, 80, 98–99

Ballmer, Ray, 99

Bank of America, 89

Bank of Papua New Guinea, 106, 110

Banks, mine development loans, 16, 24, 54. *See also* Export–Import Bank of Washington.

Barapinang Enterprises Ltd., 120

Bechtel Corporation–Western Knapp Engineering, 101; training program, 102

Billiton, B. V., 54

Bougainville (island), Papua New Guinea, 78; agriculture, 102–104; secessionist movement, 99

Bougainville Copper Ltd. (BCL), 89; BCP contract renegotiation, 31, 32–33, 88, 127–132; distribution of earnings, 104–109; dividends, xix, xxii, 84, 90, 97, 98, 105, 106, 108, 112, 122, 123, 124, 131, 132; equity holders, xxi, 89, 112, 115, 122, 123; foreign exchange operations, 106; impact on PNG economy, 100–121, 119–120; local purchases, 87, 102, 103, 105, 107; 108, 119–120; loan repayments, 90, 102, 124; scholarship program, 116; tax regime, 113–115; training programs, 102, 116, 118–119, 130. *See also* Bougainville Copper Project agreement; Bougainville Copper Pty. Ltd.

Bougainville copper mine, xiii, xvii, 135–136; area, 86; capital expenditures, xviii, 14–15, 81, 82, 89, 102, 106, 108; debt–equity ratio, xx, 24, 90; employment policies, 87, 100–101, 116, 118–119, 129; exploration and evaluation, 78–79, 81, 88, 92–94, 122; financing, 88–89, 108, 135; gold and silver content, 79, 90, 126, 135; incentives, 135; infrastructure, 79, 85, 102, 112, 135; mining leases, 81, 82, 86, 104, 131; occupation fees, 82, 86, 104, 105, 112; opposition, 81, 99; ore body, 79; model, 92; political risks, 82, 95, 99; predevelopment costs, xviii, 79, 94, 122; production, 90–91, 107, 123, 135; profitability, 32, 93–94, 95–98; rate of return, 95, 97–98, 122–126; retained value, xxi, 35, 104–109; royalty payments, 81, 82, 84, 86, 104, 112; sale contracts, 16–17, 90, 93, 94, 97, 121; smelter and refinery, 87, 121, 128, 130; taxes,

Bougainville copper mine (*cont'd.*)
xxii, 9, 32–33, 80, 81, 83–85, 88, 98,
108; 112, 112–115, 128, 130, 131,
132, technical problems, 79
Bougainville Copper Project (BCP)
agreement, 80–88; assurances
against expropriation, 82, 88; compensation to locals, 82–83, 86; employment conditions, 87; government participation, 83, 85–86;
import duties, 83; leases and royalties, 82–83; parties, 80, 82, 135;
renegotiation, 31, 32–33, 88, 127–
132; taxes, 83–84, 113–114, 126.
See also Bougainville Copper Ltd.;
Bougainville Copper Pty. Ltd.
Bougainville Copper Pty. Ltd., 98;
formation, 79; government equity
holdings, 83; mining leases, 82. *See
also* Bougainville Copper Ltd.; Bougainville Copper Project agreement
Bougainville Mining Ltd., 79, 98, 122
Bougainville Non-Renewable Resource
Fund, 131

Capital, xviii, 4, 7, 24; Bougainville
project, 88–89, 135; equity, xviii, xx,
8, 23, 29; estimating requirements,
61–62; loan, xviii, 14, 18, 21–22, 29;
Toquepala project, 40–44, 47–48, 58,
62–63, 64, 72
Capital consumption allowance, xxi, 6–
13. *See also* Amortization; Deple-
tion; Depreciation.
Cash flow, 5, 8, 9, 10; analysis, 6–18,
26–27, 122; Bougainville, 122–126;
Toquepala, 73, 75, 76–77. *See also*
Rate of return.
Central Reserve Bank of Peru, 47, 52
Cerro Corporation, 31, 43, 47
Cerro de Pasco mine complex, Peru,
39, 40, 41, 58; expropriation, 31,
54; strikes, 14
Chase Manhattan Bank, 16, 54
Chile, labor strikes, 14; nationalization
of resources, 19, 99
Comunidade de Compensación Minera,
55
Computer, mine evaluation, 92
Contract negotiation, xvii, 13–14, 24–
29, 66; bargaining strength, xxii, 25,
30, 31; conflict, xxii, 31–33; interna-
tional standards, 26, 32; objectives,
24–25; political factors, 30, 32; renegotiation, xxii, 29, 30, 32–33, 132

Conzinc Riotinto of Australia (CRA),
Bougainville project, xvii, 78–80, 88,
89, 94–99; BCP agreement objectives, 81–82; dividends, 122, 123,
124, 126; equity holdings, 89; projected returns to, 97
Copper prices, 33, 49, 50, 60, 65, 73,
75, 94, 95, 97, 123, 132; projection,
xix, 4, 15–16, 59–61; relative, 107
Cuajone copper mine, Peru, 39, 40, 41,
50, 65, 68; capital expenditures, 53,
61, 67; development agreement, 20,
31–32, 46, 51–53; financing, xx,
xxii, 24, 31, 46, 50, 52, 53–54, 55,
65, 72, 73, 75, 76, 77; political factors, 54; production costs, 54; sales
contracts, 53

Debt–equity ratios, xx, 21, 24, 58,
90
Debt service, xx, xxi, 4, 10–11, 14,
22, 81, 98, 124
Defense Materials Procurement Agency
(DMPA), 40, 41, 44, 59
Defense Production Act, 41, 42, 43,
47
Defense Production Administration
(DPA), 41
Depletion allowances, 11–13, 58, 65,
70
Depreciation allowances, 7–11, 70. *See
also* Accelerated depreciation.
Developing countries. *See* Host coun-
try; *and specific country*.
Discounted Cash Flow (DCF), xxi,
5–6, 7, 9, 10; Bougainville mine, 95.
See also Rate of return, internal.

Empresa Minera del Peru (Minera
Peru), 47, 51, 54
Equity. *See* Capital; Rate of return.
Ertsberg copper project, Indonesia, 21,
135–136
Espie, Frank, 99
Export–Import Bank Act (1945), 41
Export–Import Bank of Washington,
xix, 16, 24; Bougainville loan, 89;
Toquepala loan, 41, 42–44, 46–47,
48, 50, 59, 62–63, 65, 72
Expropriation and nationalization,
xix–xx, 29–30, 31–32, 54, 99

Foreign exchange, 19–20, 25, 46–47,
52, 70, 99, 111

Foreign investment, economic factors, 3–18; impact on host country, xvii, 66, 70, 71, 100–121; political factors, 18–20, 57, 82, 95, 99; spreading the risks, 20, 25. *See also* Contract negotiation; Mine development.
Freeport Indonesia, 21
Frei, Eduardo, 19, 99

Garnaut, Dr. Ross, 130
Germany, 17
Gold, 78, 79, 90, 107, 126, 135; prices, 123
Goodwin, R. F., 44
Government Investment Corporation, Papua New Guinea, 89

Hoskold formula for mine valuation, 5
Host country, benefits from foreign investment, xvii–xxi, 34–35, 66; capital expenditures, 22, 29; contract negotiation, 18, 25, 27, 31, 34; contract renegotiations, xxii, 28, 33, 132; contract violation, 30, 32; equity holdings, 23, 26, 28; expropriations and nationalizations, xix–xx, 29–30, 54, 99; investment climate, xix–xx, 18–19, 28, 30; mining contracts, 34; profit calculation, 5–6; resource exploration, 25; sharing before tax earnings, 28, 69; unworked concessions, 21, 55

Ilo, Peru, smelter, 49, 50
Import duties, 16, 46, 52, 83
Incentives, 135; depletion allowances, 11–12, 70
Indonesia, 21
Infrastructure, 22, 29, 66; Bougainville mine, 79, 85, 102, 112, 135; Toquepala mine, 58
Interest rates, 22, 95
International Center for Settlement of Investment Disputes (ICSID), 28
International Chamber of Commerce, 88
International Finance Corporation (IFC), 54
International law, 30, 127
International Petroleum Company, 57, 99
Investment insurance, 20, 27, 82

Japan, 17, 90; loans, 89

Kennecott Copper Corporation, 6, 31
Kennecott Pacific Pty. Ltd., 5–6, 14

Kobuan, Papua New Guinea, agricultural experimental station, 104

Labor, profit sharing, 55; strikes, 14, 49, 50; training programs, 102, 116, 118–119
Land restoration, 104
Landowners, local, payments to, 82, 86, 104, 105, 112
Lapun, Paul, 81, 99
London Metal Exchange (LME), copper prices, xix, 15, 16–17, 59, 61, 75, 90, 94, 95, 97, 98, 132

Mawby, Sir Maurice, 99
Mine development, xiii; capital outlay, 14, 20; economic factors, xix, 3–18; estimating costs, 4, 14; financing, 4, 14, 20, 21–24; predevelopment costs, xviii, xxi, 11, 13, 24; profitability, 3–6, 13, 32; tradeoffs, 13, 20, 22. *See also* Contract negotiation; Foreign investment.
Mining Communities (Comunidades Mineras), 54, 55–56, 68, 69, 71, 75
Monte Carlo model of calculating rate of return, 17

National Advisory Council on International Monetary and Financial Problems (NAC), 41, 43
Net Cash Flow (NCF), 6, 19, 33; Toquepala, 73–75, 76–77
New Broken Hill Consolidated Ltd. (NBHC), 79, 88, 89, 94, 95, 96, 97, 122
Newmont Mining Corporation, 43, 47
Northern Peru Mining and Smelting Company, 40, 58
Notman factor, 63

Odría, Gen. Manuel, 44, 57
Ok Tedi copper project, Papua New Guinea, 6, 14, 121
Open-pit mines, 58; investment requirements, 24
Ore body, evaluation of, 13, 15
Ore processing, 16–17
Overseas Private Investment Corporation (OPIC), 20, 27

Paley Commission Report, 40, 60
Papua New Guinea (PNG), 6, 14, 31, 78, 80; apprenticeship system, 118; Bougainville equity shares, xxi, 83, 89, 108, 112, 115, 123, 128, 130; BCP contract renegotiation, 127–

Papua New Guinea (PNG) (cont'd.)
132; capital outlay, 85, 102, 112,
115, 117; economy, 109–111; foreign exchange income, 99, 111; impact of Bougainville project, 100–
121; investment climate, xix–xx, 80,
82; mining laws, 80–81; revenues
from Bougainville, xx–xxi, 82, 112,
124; tax laws, 80, 81, 83
Papua New Guinea Development
Foundation, 105
PDF Holdings Ltd., 120
Panguna Development Foundation
Ltd. (PDF), 120
Panguna Development Wholesale Pty.
Ltd., 120
Percentage depletion, 11–12
Peru, Cuajone bilateral agreement, 46,
51–53; expropriations, 31–32, 54,
99; investment climate, xix–xxii, 57;
labor strikes, 14, 49, 50; mining
laws, 44, 45, 46, 55, 57; Quellaveco
agreement, 46, 55; retained value
from Toquepala, xx, 50, 67–69,
70–71; tax laws, 65; Toquepala
mining agreement, 41, 43, 44–47;
unworked concessions, 21, 55
Phelps Dodge Corporation, 43, 47
Price projection, copper, xix, 4, 15–
16; Toquepala project, 59–61
Profitability, xvii, xx, 3–4, 13, 32;
measures of, 5–6. See also Rate of
return.

Quellaveco mine, Peru, 39, 40, 44,
47; capital expenditures, 61, 72; development agreement, 46, 55; rever-
sion to government, 55

Rate of return, 26, 126; accounting, 5,
75, 76, 77; internal, xxi, 5, 7, 8, 9,
10, 19, 24, 27, 73–75, 96–97, 129,
133; minimum expected, xvii, xix,
17–18, 21, 27. See also Discounted
Cash Flow.
Rents, xvii; division of, 28, 129
Retained value, xxi, 34–35; Toquepala
mine, 66–69, 105, 109
Rio Tinto-Zinc Corporation, 79
Ross, Anthony Clunies, 130
Royalties, 26, 29; Bougainville, 81, 82,
84, 86, 104, 112

Selebi–Pikwe Mine, Botswana, 135–
136

Silver, 49, 50, 79, 90
Smelters and refineries, 16–17
Southern Peru Copper Corporation
(SPCC), xvii, xxii; Cuajone bilateral
agreement, 20, 31–32, 46, 51–53;
formation, 41; Quellaveco agree-
ment, 46, 55; profitability, 65;
stockholders' returns, 72–75; Toque-
pala agreement, 39, 44–47, 48, 51,
55. See also Toquepala copper
mine.
Southern Peru Copper Sales Corpora-
tion, 51, 53
Spain, 90
Standard Oil Company, 57
Stanford Research Institute, 16
Stewardson, Dr. B. R., 96, 97, 98
Straus, R. W., 44
Straightline depreciation, 7–8, 9

Taxes, xxi, 18, 26, 27, 29, 32–33, 114–
115, 128, 129, 132; Bougainville tax
regime, 83–85, 88, 112, 113–115,
130–132; deferred, 9–10, 45, 131;
dividend transfer, 45; excess profits,
45, 130–131; export, 45; tax holiday, 9, 18, 32, 98, 113, 129, 131;
Toquepala regime, 45–46, 52, 65;
withholding dividend transfer, 98,
115, 131. See also Capital consumption allowance.
Toquepala copper mine, Peru, xiii, xvii,
39–56; accounting rate of return,
75–77; capital consumption allowances, xxi, 45–46, 70, 75; capital
requirements, 40, 41–42, 47, 58, 61–
62; consular fees, 46, 52; debt–
equity ratio, xx, 24, 58; depletion
allowance, 12, 72, 73; distribution
of gross revenues, 67–68; dividends, 50, 70, 72; evaluation, 40;
exploration, 39–40; feasibility, 42,
47; financing, 40–44, 47–48, 62–63,
64; foreign exchange, 46–47, 52, 70;
infrastructure, 58; labor, 70–71;
strikes, 49, 50; mining agreement,
41, 43, 44–47; political considerations, 40, 43; production, 39, 48–49,
61; production costs, 49–50, 62;
profitability, 61, 62–65; rate of return, xix, xxi, 63, 65, 73, 75; resource impact, 71; retained value,
xxi, 34–35, 66–69, 70–71; smelter,
49, 50; taxes, xx, xxi, 45, 52, 65,
68, 69; wages, 68, 69

Tradeoffs, 13, 20, 22

Union Miniere, nationalization, 99
UN Economic and Social Council, 25
United States, copper consumption,
   59; copper imports, 40; depletion
   allowances, 11; foreign policy, 43;
   import duties, 16; loans, xix, 40,
   41, 42, 47, 58; tax liabilities, 29

Vernon, Donald, 99

Villegas, Juan Oviedo, 39

Wages, 14, 102
Wells, Louis T., Jr., report, 128–130
West Germany, 90
Western Knapp Engineering, 101, 102
World Bank, 22, 24, 43, 44

Zaire, 14, 99
Zambia, 14, 26, 99; mining laws, 12–
   13